42 Days to Wealth, Health and Happiness

Also by Robin Sieger

Natural Born Winners
You Can Change Your Life Any Time You Want

42 Days to Wealth, Health and Happiness

Robin Sieger

arrow books

Published by Arrow in 2006

1 3 5 7 9 10 8 6 4 2

First published in the United Kingdom by Arrow in 2006

Arrow
The Random House Group Limited
20 Vauxhall Bridge Road, London SW1V 2SA

Random House Australia (Pty) Limited
20 Alfred Street, Milsons Point, Sydney
New South Wales 2061, Australia

Random House New Zealand Limited
18 Poland Road, Glenfield
Auckland 10, New Zealand

Random House (Pty) Limited
Isle of Houghton, Corner of Boundary Road & Carse O'Gowrie
Houghton 2198, South Africa

The Random House Group Limited Reg. No. 954009

www.randomhouse.co.uk

A CIP catalogue record for this book is available
from the British Library

Papers used by Random House are natural, recyclable products made from wood grown in sustainable forests. The manufacturing processes conform to the environmental regulations of the country of origin

Typeset by Palimpsest Book Production Limited, Polmont, Stirlingshire
Printed and bound in Great Britain by Bookmarque Ltd, Croydon, Surrey

ISBN 0 09 947858 7

To Gwen, a wonderful nurse who loved her patients
and opened my heart to life

Testimonials

Lorraine Oliver, 39, Essex, England

Ever felt that even if you cut yourself into a million pieces there would still not be enough of you to go around? You run from one thing to another and one person to another sorting, soothing with never a moment for yourself. You exist and the people around you are happy but you feel discontent? Then Robin's book is for you! I'm recently divorced, work full-time in a demanding career, financially support and care for two children. Successful in my career but I was miserable. I took up this challenge and gave myself back one hour a day to focus on me. I had neglected to care for me in all my 'busyness'. In the challenge I set priorities, focused on the 'things' that matter to me and found peace. Not easy and I stumbled along the way but my soul is much happier. I have accomplished more than ever before as I have some clear achievable goals. Go on try it for yourself!

Jeroen Blauwhoff, 41, Germany

I have read numerous books before from all the famous authors about personal growth, motivation, positive thinking. This knowledge helped only temporarily, before the old patterns of behaviour reappeared. I then read *42 Days to Wealth Health and Happiness*, and took the 42-Day Challenge and I can tell you, this book has changed my life. I have found a new and interesting job in a very positive environment, I am much more optimistic about the future, my family life has improved, I am healthier, I have lost weight, I am more relaxed and every morning when I get up I embrace the world. I can recommend this book to everyone.

Nikki Cameron, 47, Scotland

This book is about a journey. It will take you deep inside yourself and you will emerge having learned more about what you are capable of, what you want out of life and how to reach goals that you may have last dreamed of years ago and then forgotten. This book came at a time in my life when I'd been given an opportunity to live a completely different life – the only trouble was that I had no idea what that different life should be. The 42 days gave me time out to focus on what was really important to me. Living with targets that challenged mind, body and soul taught me that I could change direction without fear. Don't do this if you think it's a magic wand – life will still get in the way during the 42 days and there will be days when you are convinced that only a strong coffee and a really big piece of cake will get you through!

Helen Clark, 37, England

The 42-Day Challenge has encouraged me to put my life on track. I now feel healthier and happier because of it. I looked forward to reading the daily reflections each morning which helped guide my thoughts and actions. Setting goals and making a conscious effort to impact on others with compassion and a positive attitude are skills that I intend to continue throughout my life. I now feel more peaceful and content than ever before and have learned the skills to achieve this. I recommend this book to anyone who is looking for renewal and a sense of excitement at what the future may hold for them.

Lorraine Earle, 53, London, England

Before taking part in the challenge, I lived my life feeling I was always in a rush, always having to be doing something or I would feel guilty. This resulted in very low energy levels by the evening time and I actually achieved very little outside of business hours, I just felt exhausted. I now feel calm and centred and I have lots more energy. I have lost weight and achieved various things from the challenge but the main benefit is how I feel inside. I am in control of my life now by making choices rather than just reacting and I now understand that the feeling of security comes from within. Anyone who takes up the 42-Day Challenge will definitely benefit from it.

Sally Hasson, MBA, 40, California, US
If you are ready for a life-changing experience, this is it! It will change your outlook, your marriage, your parenting skills, your professional life, etc.! If I can do it, so can you! The 42-Day Challenge combined working on my body, mind, and spirit. That is what worked for me. I wasn't just concentrating on trying to lose weight or just learning something new. I lost 16 pounds on this programme. I have gained so much confidence in myself and my abilities because I realise, from Robin's book, that I can change any time. It's up to me. No excuses. Although I had heard that before, it hit home and stuck because I was improving the whole me. I have vowed to make this programme an everyday programme for me. Go on. Take the leap of faith and change . . . only you can make the change for the better for yourself.

Lynn Hidy, 38 Syracuse NY, US
If you are picking up this book because you want to improve your life, don't put it down! I took the 42-Day Challenge to prepare myself for a huge life change – moving to a new state, starting a new career, along with the potential of role changes within my marriage. It seemed overwhelming. Robin helped me walk through all aspects of my life, take small daily steps towards my goal, and helped me reflect on who I want to be as a person. You have to work daily to change your own life – this book will keep you company and give you focus and direction. Take action, buy this book, follow the 42-Day Challenge, and change your life for ever.

Sara Lander, 38, New York City, US
Taking the 42-Day Challenge has had a positive and direct impact on my life. Robin's programme gave me the confidence to trust myself and the universe, proving that life does not need to be that

difficult! And although weight loss wasn't a goal, I've been told that I look great and the fit of my clothes confirms the talk. I believe the completeness of the programme is what makes it work and taking any one portion of the programme without the others would not have resulted in the dramatic changes that I encountered. I've incorporated many of the practices into my life on an ongoing basis . . . it is that important to me!

David Madley
I started the 42-Day Challenge as I had a life I didn't want, dreading going to work, failing to achieve the results I wanted, coming home tired and stressed-out, unable to enjoy any home life and brooding on the day that had gone, bingeing on sweet snacks between meals. Having committed to the 42-Day Challenge I now have a life again and am starting to achieve those first steps en route to being able to pick up my old hobbies and pastimes. And I now can choose to have the life I want. Having read several self-improvement books and not moved forward, I have found that *42 Days to Wealth, Health and Happiness* has shown me how to apply those life-improving skills in a way that works for me. If you are prepared to commit yourself wholeheartedly to improving your life then the 42-Day Challenge is where to start.

Mark Mortimer, Surrey, England
The biggest thing I got out of *42 Days to Wealth, Health and Happiness* was the ability to break bad habits and replace them with good ones, I learned that if you want to, you can change your life and do anything.

Dick Taylor, 52, Lititz PA, US
I believe Robin has uncovered a simple plan for diet, exercise, enlightenment, growth and personal achievement that anyone could be successful with.

This is not a weight-loss book, but you will lose weight. It's not an exercise programme, but you will become fit. It's not a motivational book, but it will motivate and inspire you with new thinking. The 42-Day Challenge is about you as a whole person. And it will create positive change in every aspect of your life.

For me, taking the challenge meant losing close to 20 pounds, getting the exercise habit and doing daily unconditional acts of kindness. It also meant setting goals in my personal life and achieving them, daily meditation to focus myself each morning and journalising my journey both to keep that focus and measure my daily progress.

The challenge has provided me with a solid foundation upon which I will continue to build and improve my life. No matter what age you are, you CAN change for the better. But only if YOU want to! If you sincerely want to improve your life, this book will take you there.

Robin Wheeler, England
This is definitely not a book for the faint-hearted. But if you, like I was, are stuck in a mental and physical rut with nothing good happening to you and always feeling tired and restless – BUY THIS BOOK! There are very few books that are genuine life-changers, this most definitely is one.

Ash Latif, Staffordshire, England
Do you find yourself at a crossroads in life? Do you want to transform your health, wealth and outlook in life? If the answer is an overwhelming YES, then this book is for YOU. Robin will take you on an incredible 42-day journey which will transform your outlook on life and the things which are most important to you.

Andy McCann, 39, Cardiff, Wales
You really should try the 42-day programme. You cannot doubt your ability to complete it more than I did before I started it. I began the challenge twenty months after my life as a physical education teacher was turned upside down when I suffered an unexpected stroke. The trauma of the stroke took away my confidence and left me with physical difficulties.

The 42-day programme challenged me in every way. That said,

the hardest part is simply making the decision to start it. I hope you do, but be prepared, as it is actually a programme of indulgence, not of restriction. Your body will be provided with real energy, your self-esteem will be provided with real feelings of self-worth, and your goal-setting approach to life will become real and dynamic. What a way to go through life!

Rosamond M. Deegan, MBA, 32, England

Robin's 42-Day Challenge has been a total revelation for me. I am quite cynical about 'change your life' genre books, but following Robin's straightforward guidelines enabled me to set my own agenda and reduce stress at work during a time of extreme pressure, and also drop a dress size. Most importantly the challenge has created an opportunity for me to focus on what I really want to get out of life. In my opinion, the daily reflections alone justify the cover price.

Eve Eighmy, 59, Kansas City, US

Change my life in 42 days? When I read about the 42-Day Challenge in *Sieger Sense*, Robin Sieger's email newsletter, I decided to accept the challenge. Robin's plan for meditation, diet and exercise was just what I needed to break out of the monotony of old bad habits. All I can say is – this really works! I feel fitter, became mellower in my outlook and actually like my fellow humans more. Even if you don't think you need to take the challenge – *especially* if you don't think you need it – this is one plan for mind, body and spirit that really works.

Fiona McTaggart, 32, East Kilbride, Scotland

The biggest thing I've got out of taking the 42-Day Challenge is a feeling of achievement. The fact that it's also beneficial to my physical fitness and appearance is a bonus! I've always had the best of intentions, but put things off so many times in the past. *42 Days to Wealth, Health and Happiness* has shown me how to support myself in life – it seems like a small thing but when you haven't achived anything in your life and everything starts to change for the better, you realise it's a big giant thing! Thanks v. much Robin.

Foreword

I meet people who have immersed themselves in personal development and self-improvement literature, they have attended courses and workshops, they are wonderfully knowledgeable, and ironically have not moved one step closer to the realisation of their goals over the years, and, I am sorry to say, are never going to.

It is not through lack of desire, intention or motivation that they fail, rather they simply don't take action. The reason they don't take action is because they never had an effective plan to take action from in the first place.

Every journey requires a starting point and a destination, otherwise you will end up wandering aimlessly and get lost. In life I meet many who with the best intention in the world are wandering aimlessly and are hopelessly lost.

I have written *42 Days to Wealth, Health and Happiness* as a call to action for you, to learn how to 'create an effective plan for success'. To turn knowledge into action, and action into results, results that you and others will see in 42 days. I have turned it into a modern-day challenge. It will change your self-perception, build your confidence and give you a feeling of achievement that few will ever know.

Robin Sieger
London

Overview

Banish the failure habit

Very few of us are taught how to be successful. Most of us, though, unwittingly learn how to fail, to the extent that it becomes a habit. It is this 'failure habit', ingrained in each and every one of us at some stage in our lives, that is responsible for diets not working and exercise regimes being abandoned. It is responsible for us giving up on relationships and not having the courage to pursue the careers or lifestyles we truly desire.

Not only do we repeatedly fail, but we have low expectations of ever being successful and living the lives of our dreams. We harbour the failure habit that whispers at the back of our subconscious mind, 'You're going to fail.' Failure becomes our real expectation, not success.

How many people start diets never to complete them? The dieting industry is a multi-billion-dollar business worldwide, so is the fitness industry. If that proves nothing else it proves one thing: people want to be slimmer and people want to be fitter. **People generally fail in life because unwittingly, at a subconscious level, they plan to fail.** To be more accurate, they don't plan at all. Even though they think they are in control, they are not even close to being in real control.

Give me 42 days of your life and I will help you create the future you want. This is at the heart of my challenge to you. It is my conviction and belief that if you take control of 42

days of your life – that's just six weeks, taken one day at a time – then you will engage your mind, your body and your spirit in such a way as to create new habits for the rest of your life.

How to use this book

This book is designed to help you overcome the failure habit. It is designed to put you back in control by starting with small incremental goals and helping you feel good about yourself for life. It is based on addressing the three qualities that make us uniquely human: the mind, body and spirit.

The mind – easy-to-follow daily exercises in meditation and visualisation to help you gain inner peace and future success
The body – easy-to-follow exercise and healthy eating plan.
The spirit – a series of 42 daily reflections to help you rediscover your life.

The Perfect Hour – 60 minutes will change your life for ever

This is the time you will give yourself each day of the challenge, first thing in the morning, to still your mind, prepare your thoughts, review your goals and establish plans for the future.

Though the challenge is for 42 days, I think it could have been called 42 hours, because if you really commit to the first hour of the day, every day, I promise you, you will succeed.

The 7 rules for the 42-Day Challenge

- Meditate and visualise for 20 minutes every morning as part of your 'Perfect Hour'
- Exercise every day for at least 20 minutes
- No smoking
- No alcohol
- Perform an act of unconditional kindness every day
- Think positively and believe in yourself at all times
- Don't eat processed, convenience or junk foods

42 Days to Wealth, Health and Happiness

Contents guide

The 42-Day Challenge is set out in three sections designed for easy use so that you can refer to it at all times

Part 1

Tells you why I created the 42-Day Challenge, what it did for me and what it will do for you.

How to make the 42-Day Challenge work for you. I explain the easy-to-follow practical steps you take:

7 rules for successfully completing the challenge:

- **Meditate** and visualise every morning for 20 minutes
- **Exercise** every day for at least 20 minutes
- **No smoking**
- **No alcohol**
- **Perform an act of unconditional kindness every day**
- **Think positively and believe in yourself at all times**
- **Don't eat processed, convenience or junk foods**

Get control over your life in 24 hours
Why planning each hour really works
Start every day with your Perfect Hour
Just 60 minutes each morning – your life deserves it!
– 15 minutes to awaken fully to the day
– 20 minutes meditation and visualisation
– 15 minutes stimulating your mind for the future
– 10 minutes real-time planning for now

Manage your day in two-hour blocks to develop automatic self-monitoring of your time-management and personal goal focus.
– Countdown to the 42-Day Challenge, why it is important to plan ahead to guarantee success.

Part 2

42 daily reflections that will change the way you think, feel and experience your life. The 42 reflections are designed to give you a balanced view of areas of importance in life, by addressing all aspects of your mind, body and spirit. Each reflection will be your own thought for the day, with the intention of heightening your self-awareness and your thinking, and gradually building towards your personal transformation.

Part 3

Exercise and healthy eating plans, plus a simple meditation technique. Meditation and visualisation techniques combined with the 42-day healthy eating plan and fitness guide with 10 basic exercises.

The benefits of meditation and visualisation explained:
– Eat little and often – six times a day: breakfast, mid-morning snack, lunch, mid-afternoon snack, dinner, and mid-evening snack.
– Eight healthy-eating food groups to choose from
– Your mix and match mini-meals so you won't get bored

7 breakfasts

7 mid-morning snacks

7 lunches

7 mid-afternoon snacks

7 dinners

7 mid-evening snacks

Exercise

At least 20 minutes a day based on your personal level of fitness and preferred regime. Each week for four days focus on cardiovascular exercise and for three days focus on strength training with the emphasis on working every muscle in your body through 10 simple exercises.

My 10 basic exercises
- The push-up
- The squat
- The lunge
- The triceps dip
- The calf raise
- The sit-up
- The step-up
- The bridge
- The leg raise
- The chest raise

Now what?
The purpose of the 42-Day Challenge is to get you completely back in control of your life and raise your self-awareness of your phenomenal potential. You will change the way you think, the way you feel and how you behave – and in addition reclaim the potential you have to lead the life you want and reach your personal goals and the success you deserve.

Once you complete the 42-Day Challenge you will be firmly back on track and will have changed beyond recognition.

My challenge will transform your life – I promise

The purpose of the challenge is simply to enable you to transform your life physically, mentally and spiritually. **I want you to reclaim your personal power to develop your full potential and experience life at its highest level.** To create the personal fulfilment, success, joy and sense of purpose in life to the benefit of those closest to you that so many people never experience.

Busting myths

I want to examine a couple of myths. People frequently tell me, when I ask them why they have not managed to break the habits of a lifetime, that they *can't* change, that they've tried many times before but they just *can't*. I want you to understand that you can. You just don't believe that you can. **Your failure habit is so ingrained that you automatically assume that you can't change, and this is happening at a subconscious level.** As we go through the 42 days you will change that belief completely.

You do have time

People frequently tell me they just don't have the time. You have plenty of time; you just don't manage it. So if you tell me you can't manage your time then I want you understand this is another myth that you have perpetuated. The reality is you do have the time and I will show you how to manage it over the next six weeks.

You do have the power

Another slightly sadder excuse I regularly hear is, 'Robin, I'm weak. I just don't have the willpower.' You have the willpower to do anything you put your mind to – it's just gone soft. You've not used it to your best advantage so you've given up believing you can use it to effect real change. **You have to use your willpower constructively, to strengthen it every day – by exercising it every day, through the achievement of small incremental goals and feeling good about yourself.**

It's not too hard – in fact it's easy

Finally, the third thing I hear a great deal is, 'It seems hard.' The truth is if you really want to change you'll find it easy, if you don't then everything you do will seem like hard work.

Beat those negative habits back

As you re-establish new habits of positivism and goal-setting, the old negative habits will be fighting for their very survival. You are deconstructing and destroying them – so in a last-ditch battle for survival your intentions and your sense of purpose will all be put to the test. And this will be the battleground where you resist the temptations of the old bad habits or give in to them.

Think of this for a moment: every man or woman who has stood on the top of a high mountain or travelled incredible distances in pursuit of the unknown experiences a sense of fulfilment, purpose and heartfelt satisfaction that few will ever know. **You will experience this when you reach the end of the 42-Day Challenge and change your sense of your potential – for ever.**

Four important wins I want for you

1. I want you to wake up to the understanding that the universe which you are part of has given you all the tools you need to achieve your goals.
2. I want you to reach out, to deconstruct the self-limiting beliefs that have trapped you into believing that you will *never* change and experience success, be happy, healthy, wealthy or loved.
3. I want you to break the failure habit once and for all and replace it with the happiness habit and the personal success habit.
4. I want you to change your outlook and level of expectation in life from negative to positive. We don't fail to reach our goals in life because we are unlucky, or lack desire or motivation. **We fail because we give up, and we give up because we never had a plan in the first place.**

Part 1

But first my challenge to you!

I CHALLENGE YOU

TO FOLLOW THIS 42-DAY PLAN

TO TAKE FULL CONTROL

OF YOUR ACTIONS

TO STICK TO IT

COME WHAT MAY

AND TRANSFORM YOUR LIFE

FOR EVER.

<u>THE 7 RULES OF THE CHALLENGE</u>

1 Meditate and visualise every morning for 20 minutes
2 Exercise every day for at least 20 minutes
3 No smoking
4 No alcohol
5 Perform an act of unconditional kindness every day
6 Think positively and believe in yourself at all times
7 Don't eat processed, convenience or junk foods

The 7 rules for success

1) Meditate and visualise every morning for 20 minutes

'Learn to be silent, let your quiet mind listen and absorb'
Pythagoras, Greek philosopher, c.560–c.480 BC

There is a vast body of medical research supporting the benefits of meditation. Benefits include reducing blood pressure and slowing down your heartbeat. It is the mental and spiritual benefits, however, that will benefit you the most as you progress through each week of the six-week 42-day challenge. Meditation enables you to still your mind and start your day from a place of great peace. It requires us to do nothing, which for so many people seems impossible. You can learn to create deep calm and stillness at the start of your day wherever you are in the world. You can always find 20 minutes to sit in absolute stillness and silence, relaxing your body and stilling your mind. In meditation you will be connected to the universal consciousness; you'll be connected to the deepest peace within yourself.

You need to make time to explore the silence. **It is in the silence that you will hear the still, small voice of your intuition,** become refreshed and renewed for the day ahead. Meditation allows us to be in a state of complete physical relaxation and mental stillness. If you can keep the sense of peace and relaxation with you for the rest of the day it prevents you from getting anxious, allowing you to stay calm in times of stress. When things do go wrong, the peace you feel within will allow you to react in a controlled way and not an emotional one. It is from this position of deep mental stillness and physical relaxation that we need to visualise our goals – for the day ahead and for the long term.

2) Exercise every day for at least 20 minutes

Every day you need to do a minimum of 20 minutes of exercise. What you choose to do is up to you, and I am sure will be determined by your level of fitness. You do not have to rush out and join a gym. **What is important is to exercise every day**. In Part 3 of the book there is a 10-exercise routine which you can complete wherever you are.

---

5 immediate benefits of 20 minutes daily exercise:

- Improved mental conditioning
- Increased wellbeing
- Raised self-esteem
- Reduced body fat
- Increased energy

The more you put into exercise the more you will get out. However, the 42 days is not a fitness programme, it is about establishing a positive habit of exercise.

3) No smoking

If you are a smoker then breaking a life-long negative habit like smoking will be one of the keys to changing your life because by doing this successfully you will recognise that you can change any habit you put your mind to. Whether you are a one-a-day or a 40-a-day smoker you *must* stop. You just think you can't stop now, promising yourself that you'll do it one day. Well, this is that day. Let's be under no illusion about this, **tobacco is killing you**. If after the 42 days you decide to start again then that's your choice, but for the duration of the challenge there is no smoking of any kind.

4) No alcohol

Drinking alcohol during the plan is likely to lead you to staying up later than you planned or waking up with a fuzzy head. It can jeopardise the efficiency and effectiveness of your challenge. So, no alcohol allowed – not even on special occasions such as your birthday. Too much alcohol deceives us and alters our perception of ourselves and the world around us. It allows us to make bad decisions or deludes us into thinking that we are doing better than we really are. Again, **whether you drink one unit a week or have a bottle of whisky a day, you must stop for the duration of the challenge**.

5) Perform an act of unconditional kindness every day

The purpose of performing an act of unconditional kindness every day is to help us recognise that our actions are under our control, and if we so choose they can impact positively on others. So perform your act of kindness with goodwill, love, peace and happiness in your heart. **You'll discover that what you give in life, you get back in often unusual and wonderful ways.** How would you feel if a stranger did something absolutely and wonderfully kind for a parent or close friend? You would feel your faith in mankind renewed. You would feel delighted that your parent or friend had been the recipient of unconditional kindness. I want you to be the originator of these actions and feelings of unconditional kindness. A warm heartfelt smile, asking if another person is OK, helping a struggling mum lift a buggy, opening a door and being patient when hoards of people rush through without even thanking you, or giving up that seat for someone who needs it more than you – all are acts of unconditional and non-self-seeking kindness.

This rule forces us to engage mind, body and spirit because it is through love that you connect with others. We are connected to others through a spirit of compassion, love and kindness and this rule will allow you to discover this for yourself. Practise selflessness because it takes you out of your comfort zone. It is because you are in this comfort zone that you are not moving forward in your life. You must get out of the comfort zone and helping others is a great place to start.

6) Think positively and believe in yourself at all times

A large part of the 42-Day Challenge is taking control of *how* you think and *what* you think. If you think positively and believe in yourself at all times you will be starting from an attitude of success. **Your attitude will impact on the way you think, the way you think will impact on the way you behave, the way you behave impacts on the way you perform, and the way you perform will impact on your life.**

You must think positively, because your subconscious mind will then look for evidence to validate that belief. If you think negatively your subconscious mind will also look for the evidence to validate that belief, so that is why you must think positively at all times and believe in yourself. **Have confidence that you will succeed and complete the challenge.**

Research has shown that a child's self-image at the age of 10 is a greater indicator of their future success in life than their IQ is. So? The 42 days are also about changing your self-perception. Thought is the origin of all our actions. When we meditate deeply, we come out of that state having created clarity of thought and focus. Believing in yourself is also about believing in the achievability of your goals. This is why thinking positively means using positive language and taking positive action to become the person you want to be. The 42 days demand that you believe in yourself. **By thinking positively and believing in yourself you will discover that belief always comes before behaviour.** You were not born to fail, you were born to succeed. By choosing to be positive you enhance your ability to succeed. This is a very important concept, which must be remembered.

If you are a negative person who experiences misery, sadness and multiple failures you may find it hard to believe that you were not born that way. **If you choose to be positive you will create success, joy and happiness in your world and the world around you.**

7) Don't eat processed, convenience and junk foods

The benefits of eating healthily are well documented. Over the years there has been a massive increase in processed foods that are high in salt, fat and sugar. The body struggles with these three substances when they are present in dosages exceeding your daily requirement. The sugar can lead to diabetes, the salt can lead to high blood pressure and fat leads to weight gain. If we are going to devote 42 days to developing our minds, our spirits and our bodies it is important that we look after our bodies as well as we can. In Part 3 of the book you'll get a healthy-eating schedule that will give you a list of foods to eat and to avoid.

Would you knowingly eat something that was poisonous in the knowledge that it would kill you? Of course you wouldn't. So where possible eat fresh, if not, go frozen.

You Absolutely Must Keep a Personal Daily Journal

To keep yourself accountable to the challenge you will need to keep a daily journal, in which you write down your daily goals and measure your progress. The additional purpose is to physically tick off the actions relating to diet, exercise and your personal daily goals.

Writing down your daily goals is a dynamic technique, because it starts the process of taking action. The physical act of writing helps reinforce the goal in your subconscious mind. Therefore the daily journal becomes your conscience, to which you become accountable, making sure you follow through on what you have planned to do. This way there are no excuses for saying that it skipped your mind or that you forgot.

I would recommend a small hardback notebook. In the opening page write down the goals that you wish to have completed by the end of the challenge, additionally include goals that are much longer term with completion dates for these too.

On the left-hand page you begin with day 1, the right-hand page is for your personal notes and observations.

The reviewing, inputting of actions taken and the following day's goals will be a part of the Perfect Hour at the start of the day. By doing this you will be able to review the goals you achieved, and put a tick against the action successfully completed. You will then be in a positive frame of mind as you fill in the goals and actions to be taken for the day ahead.

So during the Perfect Hour when it comes to reviewing the previous day you are able to see the progress you made in the past 24 hours, then write down the goals for the next 24 hours.

I have kept it very, very simple, it is not a daily diary or an intricate log book. I call it the tick and dash book, because once you have ticked the boxes you can dash off and fill in your goals and must do's for the day ahead.

Example

DAY 26

Meditation and visualisation ☐

Exercise programme ☐

No smoking ☐

No alcohol ☐

Act of kindness performed ....

....

Positive thoughts, words and deeds ☐

No processed, convenience or junk foods ☐

Goals for day 26

1..................................... ☐
2..................................... ☐
3..................................... ☐
4..................................... ☐

Countdown to the Challenge

I cannot recommend strongly enough the need to plan a start date no sooner than 7 days in advance. This is not something you begin the day after picking up the book; too often enthusiasm takes over from logic and preparation, the result is always the same – chaos and early failure.

You need to plan your start date, and prepare for it mentally by counting down to it. In that time you can buy your journal, experiment with some of the eating plan, get up earlier in the morning, start doing some exercise, performing acts of kindness, going without alcohol or tobacco. In short it is better that you experience all aspects of the challenge, otherwise you may be over-whelmed. **You need to plan and prepare for the challenge for at least 7 days before you begin.**

The key to the challenge is to be ready to start it. **You have to get your mind in the right place to prepare yourself for it.** If you are giving up processed foods, smoking and alcohol for the duration, you might want to plan to go out for a dinner with friends or family or have a party in your house. You will need to stock up your fridge with healthy foods. Do you have the right clothing for exercise or is it time to buy an exercise mat?

So don't race off ill prepared for the 42 days that will transform you, **take time to think about what you want to get out of it**, the challenges you may face, and determine to be as prepared as possible. Remember **success is not a matter of luck, it is a matter of design**. So take a few days to prepare, design, then set your start date.

A Typical Day

Get control over your life in 24 hours

You may be familiar with the expression 'take care of the pennies and the pounds will take care of themselves'. This was drummed into me as a young boy growing up in Glasgow. I've heard friends from other nationalities say the same thing. I would say the same thing about your life. **Take care of the hours and the weeks, months and years will take care of themselves**. All too often we don't take care of the hours, we postpone, we procrastinate, we don't have a schedule for the day because it seems too organised. As a result we bounce around reacting to events as they happen and not being prepared – because we didn't plan.

Why planning each hour works
The common thread to military battles won and family vacations enjoyed is detailed planning. People know where they are meant to be and when they're meant to be there. We plan many aspects of our lives and yet ironically we don't plan our lives. **By creating routines and planning your day you will achieve much and you will be in control starting with an hour at a time and building to days and weeks.**

Establishing good habits and routines is critical to completing the challenge; unless it becomes unrealistic, stick to your planned schedule and tasks for the day. When travelling or on holiday you may have to adapt the schedule. It simply means you change your timetable for that day.

Visualisation

The purpose of the visualisation is to get you into a deep state of relaxation. Then when you are physically and mentally relaxed the positive images or affirmations you think about will be embedded very deeply in your subconscious mind. Then as you go through your day the deeply held thoughts will be reinforcing your self-image without you being aware. **You are in effect replacing the old software with new improved thoughts, beliefs and feelings. These will automatically assist you in changing your current way of thinking and seeing yourself.**

Use positive self-talk

We should validate our new beliefs and feelings throughout the day with short affirmations which are positive in language and content. Use positive language when you are having an inner dialogue with yourself. When you experience setbacks or failure, don't beat yourself up for being less than perfect, look for and accentuate the positive. The best way to do this is to **have a short positive affirmation that you can repeat throughout the day, especially at times when you are feeling a little low or stressed**.

Start every day with the Perfect Hour

That's just 60 minutes each morning! Your life deserves it! I travel for over a 100 days a year and my routine becomes pretty chaotic. Yet I always build in the time to exercise, meditate and visualise. I have found without any doubt that the very best way to do this is to give myself an extra hour every day by getting up one hour early. I call this the Perfect Hour. It sets the tone for the day, allows me to organise my thoughts, feelings and emotions. I often find myself using it to read an inspiring book or listen to inspiring music. **The first hour of the day sets the tone.**

Get it right and the rest of your day will follow on just as it began. The first hour of the day is the time we are most likely to have control over. The phone's not ringing, there are no workplace demands on our time from other people, no emails or documents to be read. It is your time: the Perfect Hour. You can reflect on the day ahead, meditate, visualise, plan and review.

This is your life, and if you fail to plan you are planning to fail, even though you don't know it. **Master the use of the first hour every day and you will regain control of your life.**

So, you must begin every day with the Perfect Hour of uninterrupted time to yourself. It will mean getting up one hour earlier. Though most people believe they don't get enough sleep at the best of times, you will soon discover that within the meditation you will reach deep levels of conscious relaxation that are more refreshing to the mind and body than sleep.

Your Perfect Hour

0600 – Get up, stretch, dress and become fully awake to the day.

0615 – Meditation and visualisation.

0635 – Read the daily reflection, and consider its application in your life.

0650 – Review your goals for the day, write up your journal, tick off the goals you achieved yesterday and make a goal list for the day ahead.

0700 – The rest of the day is yours from here on.

What the Perfect Hour does for you

First 15 minutes: By doing the basics of getting up in the morning: use the toilet, drink water, wash face, brush teeth, dress, etc., you become fully awake and active. Within just a few days of starting the challenge you will discover that your body becomes accustomed to this earlier start.

20 minutes meditation and visualisation for the day: Meditation is when you relax your mind and body, and in so doing maintain the feeling of calmness and relaxation throughout the day. Visualisation is important because it is where we programme the successful completion of our goals into our subconscious mind. This will quickly become your favourite part of the day and I would recommend building in an additional period of meditation and visualisation in the early evening.

15 minutes stimulating your mind for the future: By reading something every day that informs or inspires you, you are investing in your personal development. The insights you gain will shape your character. This is why I have brought together a series of daily reflections to help you begin your day. These will help you reflect on aspects of your life that may have become neglected, and will look at areas of your life beyond goal-setting and overcoming obstacles, matters closer to your heart and the soul.

Real-time planning for now: The final 10 minutes of the hour is to look at your journal or diary, to check off the goals you completed the previous day and to make your to-do list for the current day. This is where you can keep a firm check on your progress and achievements. As you progress through the 42 days, you will delight in seeing how far you have come.

Manage your day in two-hour blocks
I would suggest that you manage your day into two-hour blocks, from 7 a.m. onwards, during the 42-Day Challenge. It will help you develop an automatic way of self-monitoring your time-management and personal goal focus.

Building your confidence
This does not mean the spontaneity and fun will go out of your life. Every time you tick off an activity you planned and completed, your confidence will increase and you will feel good about yourself. You will make a mental note that you have succeeded in following

through on something you said you would do. Every time you achieve a goal, even a micro-mini goal, you set yourself, your sense of your ability to succeed grows. **The 42-Day Challenge will enable you to understand that you can grow and become the person you want to be by starting with small incremental steps.** But you have to break the habits of a lifetime that disable your sense of purpose in such a way that you fail consistently and unconsciously.

The challenge is also about developing your sense of your spirit and your mind. As you go through the 42 days, the reflections and the meditations will take you into this realm.

Example of a Typical Day

The more that you can organise and manage your time the more effective your day will be. The challenge is about putting you back in control of your life, and that is achieved by taking positive action every hour of every day. To give you an idea of how the challenge will change the way you approach the days ahead I have created this example.

0600 – When the alarm goes off don't hesitate, take immediate action, get out of bed and make that part of your morning habit. Lying in for an extra five, ten or thirty minutes is stealing time from you. It does not make you more rested, in fact all it does is reinforce the habit of procrastination and a weak will. So at the time you have planned, get up. Once you are up, stretch, dress, drink some water and become fully awake to the day,

0615 – Meditation and visualisation. The meditation is where you experience a profound sense of deep relaxation and calm; you will find as you continue the practice that the feeling extends into the rest of the day. It is also the time when you actively programme your goals into your subconscious mind. This period is the source of your taking action on your goals. It forces you to revisit every day the future goals you seek, and helps strengthen your resolve.

0635 – Read the daily reflection, and consider its application in your life. Each reflection is about aspects of our physical, mental and spiritual life, created to stimulate thought and offer understanding. It is something to meditate on throughout the day, and if it enables you to see things in a new light or encourages you to learn more, then follow your instincts and allow the reflection to resonate within you. We do not spend enough time thinking about aspects of life other than those we can see and touch. The reflections are about those intangible parts of our life that are important but frequently overlooked.

0650 – Your journal needs to become a part of your day every day, so as part of the challenge I want you to make it central to the Perfect Hour. It is where you tick the boxes in acknowledgement of all the actions you successfully completed. Then set your goal/action list for the next 24 hours. It may sound somewhat laborious but it is critical that you establish a habit of following through on your plans. It is about being able to see your progress day by day, feel good about it and build your confidence.

How you plan your day for the rest of the challenge is up to you, however, you need to eat properly, exercise daily and perform an act of kindness. I suggest always planning your exercise and diet the day before, but allowing your acts of kindness on some days to be spontaneous; on other days they can be planned in advance, because it is the act that is important, not the spontaneity.

0700 – Exercise – if possible at the same time each day. I prefer to get the exercise done early in the morning before I shower. The exercise programme for the challenge is only 20 minutes a day: four of those days it is aerobic exercise (brisk walking or running), three of the days it is the 10 resistance exercises (you will find these in Part 3).

0720 Shower followed by breakfast.

0800 Get with the plan. Every day you will have set personal goals that relate to your health, work, relationships – in fact, whatever area of your life you are changing. Therefore, every day you should have set yourself a to-do list of small goals that you have to accomplish. It does not matter how small these goals are, the important thing is that you achieve them. So by 0800 in the morning you have already done all the planning and preparation for the day, meditated, taken exercise, eaten well, are feeling great, and are ready for action.

1000	**Mid-morning snack (see Part 3)**
	Stay with the plan and continue to work through your goals for the day
1230	**Lunch (see Part 3)**
	Stay with the plan and continue to work through your goals for the day
1530	**Mid-afternoon snack (see Part 3)**
	Stay with the plan and continue to work through your goals for the day
1830	**Dinner (see Part 3)**
	Stay with the plan and continue to work through your goals for the day
2100	**Evening snack (see Part 3)**

As you will see the first two hours of the day are critical to setting up the next twenty-two hours. The timings shown are just an example of how to schedule your day. There is no right or wrong way, simply the way that fits in with you; however, **you must have a schedule to work from every day.**

Part 2

Daily Reflections

Time

'All that really belongs to us is time; even he who has nothing else has that'

Baltasar Gracian, Spanish philosopher, 1601–1658

We don't think of time as a commodity the way we think of gold, diamonds or other material assets that we can transfer to money. But time is the most valuable thing we have and we often overlook that fact and take it for granted. We just assume that there's going to be lots of it in our life but, in reality, once we are born we do not accumulate time, we lose it. The clock starts counting down, and it's only later in life that we really recognise the truth of that statement.

> Time once gone never returns – so don't waste it or take it for granted

Time is not our enemy, in fact it is our ally if we use it well and manage it correctly. It is a wonderful asset. On the other hand bad time-management is a dream-killer. It stresses you out, it gives you little freedom, you become its slave as you are running against the clock, not getting things done; it's a terrible position to find yourself in. **The tragedy is that time-management is very easy to get right.**

> Manage your time and you manage your life. Don't manage your time and it's chaos

Put a price on time

Many of you will have had the experience of flying on a scheduled airline. You buy a ticket. When you buy the ticket you know the time of departure and time of arrival. With this information you are now able to manage your journey, and if you miss the flight – tough luck. They're not going to wait for you.

The lesson of the airline ticket seems to be missed by so many people. You can put a value on an airline ticket and the consequences of not turning up on time, but in life you assume that somehow it doesn't matter because you can do it later, or it will sort itself out. Well, let me give you a bit of shocking information: it really does matter because the moment you have never comes back.

There are some people who are bad time-keepers. Their entire life they say, 'I'm always late, my family have always been bad time-keepers' – somehow justifying their actions by not taking personal responsibility for their time management. We choose to manage our time effectively or ineffectively. There are no excuses.

As you progress through the 42-Day Challenge you will recognise that managing your time is a critical part of your life success. **The only way you can measure your progress towards the goals you have set yourself is by measuring it against a time-frame**. So it is only against the calendar that you're accurately able to measure progress. Set a start date, a finish date and intermediary dates along the way to measure your progress.

The myth about time

One of the greatest myths is that we have tons of time. When we are children there is no awareness of time, things are done for us and we think we're going to live for ever. As we progress through life we realise the clock is counting down. And yet we still put things off. We still procrastinate. We still convince ourselves we've got tons of time. **The time to do the things in life you want to do is right now.**

You manage your time or you waste your time. It's your choice

Time is a resource, like money, like good health, like friends; it is a resource you can use. But once gone it never, ever returns. It is amazing how often people get together and when they reminisce they don't talk about the future, they rarely talk about the present; they talk about the past, the good times gone. Well, you are in the good times right now so always make the most of it and plan good times in the future.

Think of time like water and imagine a big, big container of water that you have for a desert crossing. Would you use that to wash your hair or cool yourself down by pouring it over your head every so often and risk running out of water before you cross the desert? Or would you manage it very carefully, ration it out drop by drop and not waste any of it, because to do so would be to put your life at risk? **Not managing your time does not put your life at risk it just means the life you want is less likely to happen.**

I am all for people being free spirits, I'm not a person who believes we should live by timetables and clocks, 24 hours a day, and be so fixated on them that we cannot stop and be spontaneous. There are plenty of opportunities in life to be spontaneous. But – and this is a big but – we need to manage our time on a day-to-day basis so we know where we're going to be. It's the reason we have calendars and diaries and we make phone calls and arrange to do things, because we know if we don't manage our time it's chaos. Managing your day and reaching your goals is done one moment at a time. **The more you plan and execute actions, the more you move towards your goal, the faster you are going to get there.** Paradoxically, I always recommend that, in planning, people should work from their destination backwards.

Let's look at it another way. You have set the goals you want to achieve 42 days from the outset of the challenge. Whatever goals they are, you first clearly identify them and then you need to work back, so in 42 days if you want to have lost 12lb in weight, how much do you realistically need to have lost after 21 days? How much do you need to have lost after 10 days? What do you need to do to get your diet on track? What do you need to do after seven days, after three days? In fact you should break your goals down into short-term daily goals, which is what I do. By writing them down I am able to make constant progress, and measure against my calendar.

You can always reschedule your goals but if you don't have a schedule to begin with you can't. **The two most important questions when managing your time are these: where and when – where do you want to go and when do you want to get there?** Once you know that, you will find the how, and the how will take the form of creating a plan, the progress of which will be measured against the calendar.

How often have you wished that you could go back in life and relive a time or a moment with the wisdom and the experience you now have? Well, we know that's impossible but you do have the present moment. So don't waste it, use it to advance and maximise opportunities to achieve your goals in life.

So reflect upon the future and make full use of the knowledge that by managing your time you will create the greatest opportunity to realise your goals, and achieve the success you seek.

Manage your time
and you manage your life.

Today

Plan your schedule and stick to it.

Expectations

'Life is largely a matter of expectation'

Horace, Greek poet, 65 BC–8 BC

How many people have said to you, 'Never forget, today is the first day of the rest of your life.' The truth contained in this well-known phrase has never left me. The truth is exactly that – today *is* the first day of the rest of your life.

I want you to recognise the importance of leaving behind your past memories of failure. **How often you have failed, and to what degree you feel you have failed, is of no consequence.** Whatever goals you have set in the past and failed to achieve are not important. Hanging on to memories of failure raises your expectation of future failure. **The next 41 days is all about going forward, starting anew and making changes that work.**

If you expect failure it is almost a dead certainty that you will fail, and if you expect to succeed – it is almost a dead certainty that you will

Many people identify with their past failures and use those thoughts and memories as their template for who they think they are. This influences their level of expectation. It is natural to have self-doubt, but to repeatedly focus on your past failures is to set the scene for future failure.

Most of us have acquired the failure habit. It is

ingrained at such a deep subconscious level you just aren't aware it's there. Understand that your level of expectation will colour and influence the outcome of the next 42 days. The challenge you face is to change your expectation from some vague notion of failure to a powerful absolute conviction that you are going to succeed.

> Because you have experienced failure does not mean that you are a failure

It is important that you enter this transformational period with a positive and strong expectation of successful outcomes. Your mindset from this point forward is critically important to the ease with which you will meet challenges, maintain your discipline and stay committed.

> Your expectation has an impact on outcome

You change your life when you change your negative emotions and expectations to positive emotions and expectations. The reality is, we and we alone are responsible for our lives and we shouldn't look to other people to rescue us. We should look to ourselves. **You will discover that you do have all** the abilities, all the resources and all the tools within you to make your life happen.

So, throughout the next 41 days it will be your mental approach that will be the source of your success or your failure. When you get that right, everything else will follow. **You must believe you can.** You must believe in your ability to succeed, and make that your number one priority. I want you to remind yourself today that you are going to succeed. Your success already exists in the future and you are simply going to spend the next 41 days preparing for its arrival.

Create in your own mind a high level of expectation

- Concentrate on taking the challenge one day at a time
- You will complete the remaining 41 days come what may
- You have all the abilities required to make your life happen
- Your previous experiences and memories have nothing to do with what you are doing now and in the future

Concentrate on the here and now even as you begin this journey of a lifetime by transforming your self-image.

When you believe you can succeed, you will begin the journey.

You really do have within you
all the resources
you need to succeed in life
irrespective of what you may
have been told or have
chosen to believe.

Today

Remind yourself that past failures are
just that, 'in the past', and
not predictors of your future.

Be 100% Positive

'Cheerfulness, it would appear, is a matter which depends fully as much on the state of things within as on the state of things without and around us'

Charlotte Brontë, writer, 1816–1855

It is estimated that 80% of the skills we require to succeed in life are attitude-based. These include determination, commitment, focus, motivation, empathy, persistence and compassion. The other 20% are skills we have to acquire or are taught to us, such as technical skills and professional knowledge.

Today I want you to reflect on the impact your attitudes will have on your life experience. Today let's concentrate on the 80% attitude-based skills. Let us be clear that **your attitude is 100% under your control right now**. The $64-million-dollar question is: **is your attitude positive or negative?**

Thinking positive makes you act positive

There is sound psychological evidence to show that a positive attitude and outlook is an effective way of enabling us to maximise the probability of creating successful outcomes of our actions.

If we have positive expectations and a positive outlook on life, we experience events throughout the day and look for the evidence to validate those beliefs. The positive person will always look for information that validates their positive outlook. Whatever happens they will see it in a positive light. For example, if they were standing at a bus stop in the rain and a full bus went by drenching them with spray from the wheels, for an instant they would be annoyed. But within minutes they would have put it in perspective and decided to get their coat dry-cleaned. The negative person standing at the same bus stop would wonder why such things *always* happen to them. They would be interpreting the events of that action through a negative frame of mind. So **if you determine to be 100% positive in all your thoughts, in all your actions and, critically, in all your expectations you will self-select the appropriate information to enable you to keep that mood and to stay focused.**

Your attitude is 100% under your control. In your childhood you may have been exposed to negative attitudes from a parent, teachers or other adult figures, resulting in the formation of negative expectations and attitudes. If that is the case then let them go – it really is that simple.

Let go of the negative

So how do you change negative thoughts? You simply let them go. You can drop the negative baggage any time you want. It's not the responsibility of other people; it is *your* responsibility. Don't absolve yourself of having a bad attitude by saying, it's just the way I am. Somewhere along the life you have lived, you allowed yourself to stop believing that there was anything that you could do about it.

Be positive in your thoughts and your actions and your spoken word

When you let go of the negative, the successful completion of the next six weeks becomes totally achievable. By taking control of the way you think and the attitudes you hold, you will control the way you behave, and, in so doing, put control back into your daily life.

The reality is that you and you alone are the person who is going to be in charge of your thoughts, your feelings and your emotions. Keep them positive and you will start to see miracles happen in your life. It may sound obvious but the great truths of life usually are.

Do not be influenced by the actions of other people. Stay calm and positive at all times. You can listen to what they say, and let them assume for whatever reason that they are right. Do not allow them to influence how you feel about yourself.

Positive attitude leads to positive thoughts which lead to positive actions. It's that simple

Stay 100% positive at all times and in all places. When people ask how you are feeling just say, 'I'm feeling great', using positive language. Your brain registers that what you have said is true. Your subconscious mind will try to act in accordance with what it is hearing.

> You cannot be positive and negative at the same time – it's just not possible

Remember, your outlook is your choice and if you make it positive in thought, word and action you will see the change manifest in your life.

Remember

Your attitude is 100% under your control and impacts on your thoughts, which impact on your actions and subsequent outcomes.

Today

Choose to be positive in all aspects of your life.

Value Yourself

'The reason why so little is done, is generally because so little is attempted'

Samuel Smiles, author, 1812–1904

I'm absolutely sure you are beginning to feel positive and aware that you are more in control. You are doing something you have never done before: sticking to a plan hour by hour. As you do so your confidence, your self-esteem and your self-image will all grow day by day.

Today I want to reflect on the notion that you need to value yourself. You make the difference to how your life will turn out when you take responsibility for taking action to stay on course and see through the daily challenges you face.

Who is the most important person in the world to you? Well, you will probably immediately think of your partner, husband, wife, parent, your children, a best friend or someone who has a profound influence in your life. These are very good and normal answers. But I would like you to think differently. I want you to think and believe that **you are the most important person in the world**.

> You are the person who is ultimately going to have the greatest impact on your life

Importance does not mean you are egotistical nor does it mean you are vain and full of yourself. It just means that you believe that your life *is* of value.

Value yourself

Anyone who has had children or works closely with children will know how vital it is to tell them that they are important, that they are worthy and that they are lovable, loved and valued. In praising children for their achievements, from the first steps and words to learning to read and far beyond, we are reinforcing their sense of what they can achieve and giving them the confidence to achieve more. A parent, carer or teacher understands intuitively that it is important that the child believes in himself or herself.

I would like you to think of yourself as being as important in terms of the contribution you can make to the quality of your life and the lives of other people. That's what I mean by importance and is the reason we should never talk ourselves down to other people or, more importantly, to ourselves. Do not let yourself engage in negative self-talk and self-labelling. **See yourself as someone whose life makes a positive difference and is of real and lasting value.**

Your actions have consequences. When you meet another person and you have an exchange of words, your words will impact on that person. The degree to which they impact is often something we may never register or know. So we should always choose our words with a sensitivity to other people's feelings.

Simple acts of kindness that we do to other people can reverberate long after the encounter is over

You can touch the lives of other people through your thoughts and actions. That is why you must value yourself and recognise that everything you do today will make a difference not only to yourself, but to others.

Your actions not only make a difference
to your life, they make a difference
to the lives of others.

Today

Choose to be proactive, positive,
and value yourself in all situations.

Positive Affirmations

'All words are pegs to
hang ideas on'

Henry Ward Beecher,
American clergyman, 1813–1887

The most common way that we communicate with other people is through the use of language. It is how we express our thoughts and intentions. We're aware that what we say, and critically how we say it, will affect how it is interpreted by others. Many salesmen, politicians and public speakers are aware of these factors and use them to their advantage, to influence those to whom they are speaking and to maximise the impact of their message. The same is equally true when we have an inner dialogue. The language we use when we experience and interpret an event will also have an influence on how we perceive the event and how we feel about ourselves.

Keep your self-talk positive

I have regularly seen people beat themselves up when something goes wrong. They blame themselves. I've heard of people saying after a business meeting, 'I'm such an idiot; I really blew that meeting.' Well, that may be how they feel emotionally about what has happened in the meeting but it is not exactly a correct statement about *who* they are. Now, if your inner dialogue is in a negative form, you will be planting damaging thoughts in your subconscious.

Keep your inner dialogue positive, because our self-image and how we feel about ourselves is shaped by the information held in our subconscious mind. The most powerful and direct way of doing this is through 'self-talk', and the use of positive affirmations.

Use positive self-talk

When something doesn't work out, don't give yourself negative feedback. The best way to avoid this is to create a positive affirmation about yourself while acknowledging the situation. An affirmation is a statement asserting the truth. It takes the form of a simple statement which is short, succinct and positive in content. So when something goes wrong, you shouldn't say, 'I'm an idiot, I'm always going to fail' or some other equally negative statement. You should say, 'Well, that didn't work as I'd hoped for – what can I learn from it?' **Use expressions like, 'I am capable, I am competent and I am continuing to learn on my road to success.' Or, 'I am able, I am intelligent and I shall continue to seek and improve my abilities to achieve my goals.'**

However, we resist using such language because it sounds too simple, and we don't believe doing so will make any difference. The irony here is that while we have no problem acknowledging that the *negative* self-talk seems to have created the problems, we don't accept that using *positive* self-talk would solve them.

Positive thoughts create positive outcomes

When you use positive affirmations, your subconscious mind acts like a piece of blotting paper, absorbs the content of that statement and uses it to create the model of who you are and the expectations you will have for the future. Not only will you grow internally through the use of positive affirmations, you will be continually reinforcing and supporting your self-image. **Our subconscious mind does not know fact from fiction, and if we do not put in positive images, positive thoughts and positive feelings we will not create positive outcomes.**

As children we are continually given many positive affirmations. We are told on a regular basis that we are clever, that we are good, that we are brave, that we are pretty, and a host of other positive reinforcements. Our self-image becomes wholly congruent with those messages. This is the reason why by the age of four most children have a very good self-image. They believe that they are capable of doing many things. When a young child is asked what they want to do when they grow up, they may say pilot, ballerina, cowboy, soldier, superhero. Their self-image is one of great capability because generally it has been continually reinforced by parents and loved ones. However, as we get older the positive reinforcement gives way to negative messages and we are no longer treated as little children.

We create a positive self-image through positive self-talk

Using positive affirmations and self-talk

When you start actively giving yourself positive self-talk, always remember that it is about consciously developing and establishing a self-image that is positive and believes in future success. So be honest with yourself; you must not deceive yourself. If you steal, cheat and do bad things, positive affirmations will not work, because they are not congruent with what is actually happening. Your positive affirmations must be reinforced by congruent actions, outcomes and experience.

So how is your self-talk at the moment? Is it positive? Do you use esteem-building expressions? Or do you tend to beat yourself up when something goes wrong? Do you fill your mind with positive thoughts, feelings and images? In the old days of the early computer programmers they used to use the expression 'garbage in — garbage out'. If the software programme was full of errors then it would be unable to run properly. Your positive self-talk and positive affirmations are exactly that, personal software for your brain.

When I was a young and played golf, I frequently beat myself up if I missed a putt or hit a bad shot. I would tell myself that I was never going to be a good golfer. However, I realised that as long as I fed myself those negative messages, the actions that were congruent with those expectations continued to manifest on the golf course. So I changed from beating myself up to always finding something positive in the outcome, even though it may have hurt at the time. Now I've become someone who's known as a relaxed character who, irrespective of the shot I hit, never loses my temper or thumps a club on the ground. Positive self-talk has enabled me to perform on a much higher level and my golf has improved to the point that I play well and always enjoy myself.

Keep them short and simple

Your affirmations need to be short, simple, and positive. For example, 'Every day I am moving closer to my goal'. 'I am capable and competent in all my actions', 'I am a good and kind person who seeks opportunities to help others', 'I am worthy', 'I am capable'.

It is these very basic affirmations that have the greatest impact. This dialogue is for you to have with yourself using positive words and phrases.

When I have run in marathons in London and in New York, I have always been very touched by the people who see my name on my T-shirt and shout words of encouragement to me. When you see a child on a bicycle having the stabilisers taken off for the first time, I have no doubt you would tell them they could do it, you would encourage them. We can easily assist other people and yet the last person we seem to want to encourage is ourselves.

Scientific evidence suggests that the plant-ing of positive thoughts and feelings deeply impacts on performance ability and on our self-image. Why do top sporting performers invest in a personal coach? The personal coach works very hard to subtly help the player create an even more powerful self-image and encourages the player to focus on the moment while out on the court, on the golf course or in the arena. Deeply embedded positive affirmations will automatically enable the person to perform at their highest level.

The visualisation method I use is a combination of hypnotic suggestion, meditation and deep relax-ation techniques that I have come across in life. I have not invented any of these; in fact, hypnosis has been around since 1500 BC in Egypt. My father was a doctor in Scotland who used hypnosis to treat patients for certain conditions that previously had had very little success with other types of intervention.

Visualisation and positive affirmations

The purpose of visualisation is to get you into a deep state of relaxation, then you will find that when you are physically and mentally relaxed the positive phrases, images or affirmations that you use will be embedded very deeply in your subconscious mind. Then, when you are going through your day-to-day actions, they are used to reinforce your self-image without your being aware. You are, in effect, replacing the old software with new improved thoughts, beliefs and feelings. These will automatically assist you in changing your current way of thinking and seeing yourself. So it would make great sense to continue to validate those new beliefs and feelings throughout the day with short affirmations which are positive in both language and content.

Always accentuate the positive

Always accentuate the positive. **The best way to do this is to have a short positive affirmation that you can repeat over and over and over again, throughout the day, especially at times when you are feeling a little low or stressed.** You will see the effects in your life. When I was learning to skydive, I always got nervous on the flight up to jump altitude. On the flight up I would repeat to myself, 'Breathe, relax, arch.' I would smile at others in the plane, and continue to repeat those three words. Breathing helped me to relax, relaxing enabled me to arch my back and get a stable body position in the air. As a result I made excellent progress through my student jumps and beyond.

Positive affirmations and self-talk impact directly on your self-image and performance expectations.

Today

Repeat to yourself, 'Today I am moving towards my future success.'

Purpose

'Go confidently in the direction
of your dreams. Live the life
you have imagined'

Henry David Thoreau, American author,
poet, philosopher, 1817–1862

I have no doubt that there is one overriding aspect in your life that you want to change, that has become your goal and the object of this challenge. It may be to change your work, it may be to lose weight, it may be to get fit, or it may be to have a better relationship with another person. It may be a combination of many goals. It doesn't really matter what goal you seek to achieve because the main thing is that it is important to you.

When you look at your goal, realise it is simply a means to an end. The achievement of the goal will give you something. It could be more money, more love, better health, higher self-esteem, a better job, nicer home, more opportunities to travel. **Whatever it may be, the achievement of your goal will help you realise something else. It is that 'something else' I want you to reflect on today. Because that 'something else' reveals your purpose.**

Behind our goals always lies a purpose

All goals have a purpose, material, emotional or spiritual, which is why our need to discover purpose in life is paramount. **Without purpose everything loses real meaning** – there becomes little reason to pursue any particular activity or action. Your purpose will lie at the heart of the goals you have set yourself.

When you look at your goal, ask yourself: what does this give me? I believe ultimately it will not simply be things. Doubtless money and financial security will be a part of it but I also believe that health, happiness, love, joy and peace of mind will be among the purposes that lie deep behind your goals.

Do your goals fit your true purpose?

Your first question whenever you set a goal is: what purpose does it have in my life? I am asked to speak at conferences all over the world. My first question to the organisers is always the same: what is the purpose of this conference? Without understanding this, I am unable to create the appropriate content.

Many people seem to feel, for reasons best known to themselves, that all purposes must be worthy, grand and full of high ideals. Trust me, your purpose does *not* need to be profound. You don't need to be a philosopher sitting on a rock somewhere, scratching your chin endlessly, coming up with something of such immense wisdom and clarity that it will light up the world. Chances are your purpose, when you analyse it and it reveals itself, will be simple.

Your purpose becomes your source of motivation and inspiration

I have three purposes that I think about a great deal. My first is to make a positive difference to the lives of the people I meet. My second is to align myself with people who enable me to make that difference. My third is never to stop learning. With these purposes I am able to determine the goals that I set.

Without purpose we will lose our way and drift through life

Don't worry if right now you can't find purpose in your goals. You don't need to get too concerned about that. But as you think about them over the days ahead, I want you to **look at what the achievement of the goal will give you beyond the goal itself.** Reflect on what it is you want to create.

I often ask people what they would wish for if they were granted three wishes. They frequently say, 'I don't know.' But when you ask a child what they would wish for they will quickly tell you. They would wish for ice-cream mountains, they would wish for toys, they would wish for endless games to play. As adults we are more likely to say: financial security, exotic holidays and good health. What is important is to determine for yourself what your three wishes would be, and what they would give you once you achieved them.

It is our search for deeper meaning in our lives that

causes us a great deal of uncertainty in our lives. I would encourage you **always to have goals that you are looking forward to, and to look beyond these goals for the intangible qualities they represent.** Material benefits will almost always be a by-product of the true purpose that you want to realise.

Today as you go through your tasks, and your actions, reflect upon your purpose. Also reflect upon this question: what achievement in your life will bring you greatest satisfaction? Having the biggest house in the street, the most outrageous watch on your wrist, the fastest car in your town? A successful career that you never really cared about? Or would it be for the compassion you showed to other people? Would it be for the contentedness with which you lived and the peace that always seemed to radiate from you? Would it simply be your joy and your positive attitude in all places at all times? **Think about what you'd like to be remembered for.**

Our self-motivation comes from focusing on what our goals give us, not only the goal itself

In life we live in a state of impermanence, nothing stays the same. We cannot hold on to things for ever, which is why we should not be attached to things that have no permanence.

Life is about letting go and being fully alive

There is no end to the pursuit of purpose; we never arrive – we are ever-improving students in search of perfection. Reflect on the goals you have set yourself. If necessary, reset them right now, or later on today. **Reset some goals if you cannot find any true meaning behind them,** but don't do it until you are sure you have identified the real goals that give you a sense of purpose.

Your purpose is the source of your
motivation and desire.

Today

Examine your goals and ask yourself
what their achievement will give you,
and you will discover your purpose.

Passion

'Only passions, great passions,
can elevate the soul
to great things'

Denis Diderot, French philosopher and writer, 1713–1784

Today I'd like to reflect a little more on purpose, or, to be more exact, the partner of purpose – passion. Purpose on its own simply gives us a clear sense of what lies behind our goals. But to bring this purpose to life we need passion.

You must to have passion for your purpose

For me passion is simply an intense emotion or intense feeling that we have about something, which moves us to act. Today I want you to reflect on and think about what it is that you are passionate about.

In life you may have many passions, or maybe a few. We may be passionate about our family, our friends, about life. Passion is a feeling that comes with an emotion. **Passion and purpose cannot survive without one another**, yet passion needs a focus that is found in purpose. It is impossible to be passionate about nothing.

Direct your passion

You must direct your passion towards your goal along with your sense of purpose. A goal is not simply about achieving, it also is about 'becoming'. It is about becoming the person we dream of being, it is about becoming fulfilled in our lives.

Being passionate about your goal
means that when you undergo
setbacks you don't give up, you
get up and try again

Your passion will enable you to remain devoted and
dedicated to the particular goal you seek to achieve.
You must keep the goal in the front of your mind
all the time, then every action taken will be seen in
terms of moving you closer, or further away, from
that goal.

A passion for the realisation of your goal will
enable you to go beyond your fears and push yourself longer, further and higher, in the pursuit of
your success. It feels no physical pain and never dries
up. It is truly powerful, and yet so often we are not
connected to it because for all our desire, we still
hesitate and are risk averse. Be in no doubt, once
you align passion to your purpose you will become
unstoppable. You simply will not give up – ever.
Passion is an intense emotional feeling, it is not a
vague desire, it is not a good idea that you just think
about. **It is a power that drives you when others
have given up.**

Chances are your life has been full of good ideas
that never developed into much more than just
ideas. Why not? Why didn't they drive forward to
reality in your life? Was it a lack of desire and passion?

Behind the highest achievers in the world you will always find desire and passion. What is the biggest mistake people make in the pursuit of their goals? Well, there are various thoughts on this, I imagine. My thought is they simply don't have the passion or the commitment to succeed, so when disappointments come along and failures are experienced they give up or they back off.

> The satisfaction and sense of self-worth you shall feel when you achieve your goal will go so far beyond your current level of imagination as to be absolutely wondrous

You will know your purpose has passion because:

- When talking about your goal you will be genuinely enthusiastic and you will want to share the entire experience with the people to whom you speak. You will be uplifted and excited just by talking about your goal.
- Every action you take, every effort you make, will contain a sense of purpose for you. You will not feel as though there is any action

you take that has no meaning as you will find meaning in every experience. Your passionate desire to succeed will engage you fully in the activity you are undertaking.

- And finally, no matter how many early setbacks you may experience, you will never want to give up or imagine giving up. It will just not be an option.

Passion and purpose when directed
to a goal are a dynamic force.

Today

Become passionate about your life
and your dreams for the future and
manifest this in your actions.

Your Wealth

'If money is your hope for independence you will never have it. The only real security that a man will have in this world is a reserve of knowledge, experience and ability'

Henry Ford, US automobile manufacturer, 1863–1947

M ost people would rather be wealthy than poor. Wealth will insulate you from many hardships of life, whereas poverty makes us vulnerable to those very hardships. But what exactly do we mean when we say we want to be wealthy? Do we mean we want a set sum of money, say £10 million? In which case if you met somebody who had £1 billion would they be 100 times wealthier than you? It's obvious that they wouldn't be 100 times happier, or a 100 times more fulfilled. So how much money is enough?

I think we need first to analyse what we mean by wealth. For me **wealth is simply abundance**. An abundance of what we want. If we want to be happy and we have an abundance of happiness in our lives every day, then I would say we are wealthy.

Equally, I am sufficiently realistic to understand that if you walk into the bank wanting to buy a house, the manager normally asks if you have any collateral against this loan to secure the money. If you look at him or her with a big smile and say, 'Well, I'm the happiest man in the world, how's that for starters?' they'll probably press some secret button under the desktop and you will be escorted out. So I think that **there is practical wealth, and then there is what I call personal wealth**.

Wealth is personal abundance, not just money

In this reflection what I'd like to do is to look at both aspects of wealth and to make sure that

they become present in your life. Practical wealth is money. It is the accumulation of money that enables you to buy things and gives you financial peace of mind. The other wealth is the internal feeling of having abundance in your life – I refer to this as personal wealth. This abundance manifests itself in our lives as: feeling loved, being involved and appreciated, and being someone who contributes to the quality of life of others. It's a feeling that gives us great comfort and security in ourselves. **Money on its own does not make us wealthy.** True wealth is having what you want, and for those of you who believe, without doubt, that wealth will make you happy, you are probably in for one of the greatest disappointments of all.

Look at the impact that sudden wealth has had on the lives of some lottery winners. Marriages break up; they go on massive spending sprees and buy things that they can't sustain. The luxury mansions in the country, the garage full of cars that are very expensive to maintain, and from the minute you buy them, with the probable exception of the house, they depreciate in value.

So the first part of this reflection is going to look at money. In my first book, *Natural Born Winners*, I looked at the seven principles that are common to successful organisations and individuals, people who have achieved great things at a personal level and others who have achieved immense wealth. It is interesting to note that the first person who made a study of how to become rich and successful in life was Andrew Carnegie, who in 1902 was the richest person in the world. He believed that there was a practical system to the attainment of financial success.

Be aware of the importance of visualising your financial success too

It all comes down to the simplest of realisations, but so many people don't believe it, or simply can't wait for it. So I will share my story with you in the hope that it resonates with you and gives you the confidence to believe it. It comes down to this simple statement: 'You manifest in your life, what you consciously think about and focus on.' In other words: **think and believe that you will have financial wellbeing and you will create it in your life, think you will be in financial need and that too will be created in your life.**

For many years of my life I had no money, I was poor. Always struggling to meet my rent, always trying to stretch my money out, unable to afford to join my friends on holidays because I didn't have any money. When we went out to eat, I was very aware when people started ordering anything expensive, because I knew I would have to pay a share of it. And this isn't to do with being mean, because I consider myself to be a generous person; I was brought up that way. I worried about money, and my fixation was on not having money, and surprise, surprise, guess what, I didn't have money. Then I started to study the effects of positive conscious thought on wealth creation.

Poverty consciousness

I locked on to one very simple and powerful belief. I had from a young age what I called 'poverty consciousness'. I saw clearly how it had influenced my thinking, my expectations and my world. I determined at that instant to change it to 'wealth consciousness', believing beyond doubt that the money would manifest in my life.

I should point out that at the time I chose 'wealth consciousness' I was six weeks away from being unemployed and had no prospects of immediate employment. But critically (*and this is the key*) I didn't focus my conscious thought about being poor any longer, I believed I would make money and have 'wealth'. Exactly six weeks to the day of embracing this feeling into my mind and heart I had quadrupled my annual earnings.

With six weeks to go to becoming unemployed I started a consulting business in the absolute belief that from that day forth and come what may, *there would be enough money in my life*. In the first six weeks of setting up my company I had a turnover that was four times the salary I had previously been earning. My company had no track record, yet with my new-found belief I was going to meetings and walking out with contracts, each one greater than my previous annual salary. Coincidence? Well I don't believe in coincidence. So exactly what was happening?

Winning others over with your confidence

What happened to me was that I stopped thinking about scarcity and I started to think about abundance. I hope that you can grasp that concept. Your thoughts and your beliefs and what you visualise are what you will manifest in your life. Obviously you cannot spend what you don't have, but when you absolutely believe with 100% confidence and place that 'feeling' deep within your soul, you will manifest material abundance; your subconscious mind will lock on to that need and help and assist your conscious mind to find the way to do it. When I went into meetings, the belief manifested itself into my life and appeared through my new-found confidence, in the way I spoke and behaved.

We attract into our lives what we think about. That should be your mantra today – keep it close to your heart. We attract into our lives what we think about.

> Personal abundance is about having inside of yourself a strong sense of fulfilment

Powerful thinking creates wealth

We start off believing money will make us happy, money will give us the things we need. Money is simply an enabler. £10 million in gold bars on a desert island will not be as much use to you as a box of matches. Andrew Carnegie, the richest man in the world in the later years of his life, set himself the task of giving away all the money he had made and putting it back into good causes throughout the world. Libraries were given to many small towns because he believed education was essential to the development of the human spirit. He commissioned Napoleon Hill to write a book looking at the foundations of wealth: *Think and Grow Rich*. It is a personal development classic, and over 65 years later it has sold over 14 million copies worldwide. It states that your wealth will be derived from your power of thinking, the impact of your beliefs and attitudes and your connection with universal intelligence.

It is more important that you *believe* rather than simply *understand*. Sometimes understanding abstract concepts that feel 'strange' is just beyond our logical

comprehension. That the universe exists we know
for a fact — we're in it! Where did the universe come
from? I haven't a clue. How did it come into exis-
tence? I have heard the latest Big Bang theory but
it's just a theory so I'm still none the wiser; in fact,
there are many theories. We can spend too much
of our lives looking for the reason rather than
enjoying the effect.

I wish you every success as you pursue the abundance of personal and material wealth. My greatest
wish is that you use it wisely to benefit other people.
Do not allow yourself to be addicted or imprisoned
by it. **The things that obsess us and control us
will ultimately imprison us.**

Wealth is not simply about money
it is about personal and material
abundance in life.

Today

Value the abundance in your life,
and live with wealth consciousness
in your heart and soul.

Active Hope

'Hope, like a gleaming
taper's light
Adorns and cheers our way;
And still, as darker grows
the night
Emits a brighter ray'

Oliver Goldsmith, Irish playwright, 1730–1774

Do you often find yourself beginning a sentence with the words 'I hope', as in 'I hope I get the promotion . . . the new job . . . a parking space . . . a new relationship.' You get the picture? We use the word 'hope' — do we use it correctly? What do we mean by hope? It is interesting to note that hope is one of the three main elements of Christian character, along with faith and love. So hope is a big aspect of life.

This reflection is about hope. Hope fundamentally is a feeling that a desire will be fulfilled. This is its definition according to popular usage in dictionaries. Yet we frequently find ourselves using the words 'I hope' when we don't expect the desire to be fulfilled at all! So you say, 'I hope I get the job' when deep down inside you don't believe you will.

For hope to be truly effective it has to contain faith and a little bit of love. It has to endorse our deep heartfelt belief in the achievability of the success we seek, so that hope is spoken of as a feeling that all will be well.

When we lose hope we lose everything

Hope is one of the most powerful forces in our lives because it enables us to stay positive, to have faith and believe we are going to succeed. Hope does spring eternal for the optimistic person. They always believe tomorrow and the day after it is going to work out. But the person without hope gives up. It is one of the saddest realities of our life that many people who have taken their own lives in tragic circumstances had reached a point of futility, where nothing mattered. They had given up the hope that things could be better.

Hope is a powerful force, and we need to understand that we should engage hope in our lives with a positive belief that our desires and our goals will be fulfilled.

> Without taking action our hope ends up becoming little more than wishfulness

Active hope makes for success

I believe there is 'active' hope and 'inactive' hope. Inactive hope is when you use positive words but in truth you don't believe. You may say, 'I hope I win the lottery', but you don't really believe it is going to happen. In circumstances over which you have absolutely no control, hoping for something borders on a miracle having to occur. Active hope is when there is sufficient evidence in your belief that what you wish to happen *will* happen because you truly believe it is realistically possible.

Active hope is having a belief that your goals will realistically happen

Active hope is when you determine to do something with the *knowledge* that it is possible. In addition to having hopes for ourselves we can encourage the hopes and the aspirations of others. When someone tells you there's something they want to do or achieve in their lives, encourage them.

My only desire when I meet someone who tells me of their hopes and their aspirations is to increase their sense of hope, to increase their aspirations, and to turn them from being inactive to active. To move them on from talking towards *doing*.

All too often in our lives we lose hope. I believe for many of us who are engaged in the 42-Day Challenge, we've looked at this as something that we've just hoped we can do but we don't really *know* we can. **I want you to take time today to think clearly about the success and the joy you will feel when you achieve your goal at the end of the six weeks.** When you consider any challenge you face, please use active hope not inactive hope, and believe without doubt that you are going to complete the challenge. When you do, it will build and increase that feeling that the desire you seek will be fulfilled.

Never, never give up hope in yourself
or your dreams, there is always a way.

Today

Practise active hope, and believe in
the realisation of the goal.

Overcoming Suffering

'Seeing much, suffering much,
and studying much, are the
three pillars of learning'

Benjamin Disraeli, politician 1804–1881

You're well into the second week of the challenge! You are creating new habits, taking control of your life, challenging long-held opinions and beliefs. Can you feel the changes taking place within you? Other people are probably seeing them too.

This is the big week. Get through the second week and you're going to make it.

Today, I am going to reflect on overcoming suffering. We have all experienced suffering to varying degrees. For some people it's a matter of small irritations or life events. Other people are born into grinding poverty or into abusive households. They grow up without the benefits of a good education or are raised without love. Their lives are difficult.

> Our character will not be shaped by what has happened to us, our character rather is formed by what we did about the things that happened to us

I have no doubt that every one of us has experienced physical or emotional suffering. It may have been a suffering so great that at the time it seemed to know no boundary. It may have been a discomfort of such proportions that at times we thought we would be better off dead.

Sad and bad things happen

I was plagued by chronic and acute anxiety from the age of 12 for 16 years. My father died when I was just 20. I was diagnosed with cancer six months after I had been dropped from the first television series that I had been due to star in. A girl that I loved very much didn't want to be with me, because she didn't feel I would ever be able to give her the life she wanted. Each one of these events at the time was a massive body blow to my confidence and my self-esteem, and the pain was terrible. I realise now, from a perspective of experience and age, that **each one of those events shaped me into becoming the person that I am now. Held within them are lessons I learned and used in the future.**

Each and every one of us has experienced body blows that leave us reeling and thinking, 'Why me? It's not fair.' Does this sound familiar? We all experience setbacks and losses. Yet many people are simply unable to deal with them. They are imprisoned by their pain and their anger. When suffering is not put into perspective we do not overcome it, rather we feel victimised and the suffering just increases incrementally. Don't get me wrong, I would much rather my father was still alive and that many of the other events described earlier had not happened. But hold on, I wouldn't be who I am today and I wouldn't have learned those lessons. Who is to say how my life would have turned out if any of those things had not happened. We often second-guess what might have happened 'if' – and that's a waste of time.

We all experience events in life that cause us to suffer – physically, mentally and emotionally. **So how do we overcome these sufferings? For a start we don't ignore them or run away from them. We must tell ourselves, clearly and carefully, that 'this will pass.'**

This has been a great comfort to me over the years; even when I had cancer and I was grieving for my father I always had a sense that it would pass, the pain would go away. I've come to realise that events in life are neither good nor bad in themselves. At the time things that appear bad can turn out to be good, things that appear good can turn out to be bad.

I know people who have inherited great wealth. You may think, lucky them. Only three years later they are in a rehab clinic with substance-addiction problems. I know people who've landed the dream job, been promoted and sent abroad only to have their marriage fail. So, good and bad are relative terms. I doubt I would ever say suffering is good, but from suffering good things can emerge. From my father's death and from the pain of the suffering that I'd experienced in my life, I had an opportunity to change, to grow and become more aware of who I am. **Suffering is not permanent, it will pass. It is especially important to remember this if you are going through a period of pain at this moment in your life**, to understand that it is not permanent.

We don't overcome suffering by resisting it. We overcome suffering by recognising that it will pass, and seeking to take something positive from the experience

Your decisions were right at the time

When I read of actors who tell the story of how they passed on a wonderful part that became a huge hit for the actor who took it and they rue the day they turned it down, I think, what a waste of energy. They turned it down for the reason that was right for them at the time. **All you can ever do in life is to make decisions based on what feels right at the time.**

My father's death taught me that relationships are here and now experiences; that we should make them as loving and understanding as possible. To live in the moment you are with a person, to be there for that person, to let them know how you feel. **Don't postpone life.**

When something that you expected
to come your way doesn't, don't
get bent out of shape

My cancer taught me how much I loved and was loved by others. It taught me to be compassionate. It taught me never to judge other people. My anxiety taught me there is always a solution to every problem we face and to never give up until you find it. It taught me that when you run away from your problems you discover that you take them with you. You cannot run away from your problems. You must face them and overcome them. It taught me that **peace and freedom from anxiety are not places but are states of mind.**

Being dropped by the TV company taught me to deal with things as they are, not as I'd wished them to be. It taught me that what we want isn't always what we need. And from the girl who didn't want to be with me I learned that if the person you love doesn't love you back then the relationship can never be a balanced one. You should never want to be with a person who doesn't want to be with you.

If you go out of your way to avoid suffering at all costs you will not truly live, you will miss much of the experience of life

It is your spirit that enables you not to identify with your suffering. You are not just your body; you are not only your mind or your emotions. I believe we are spiritual beings, having a human experience. We are not humans having the occasional spiritual experience.

Suffering is real and it is painful, but in the final analysis it will pass, and we can take something from the experience to help us in the future. And there is a lesson contained within all suffering we experience that will serve you for the rest of your life. So look back today on the painful memories from your past and value the lesson.

Suffering is not your destiny,
and in time it will pass.

Today

Reflect on your past experiences
of suffering and value what
lessons you learned, how they have
changed you in a positive and negative
way. Then focus only on the positive.

Compassion

'Compassion is the basis
of all morality'

Arthur Schopenhauer, philosopher, 1788–1860

One of the key rules of the 42 days is to perform a random act of kindness every day. **It is a wonderful thing when we extend kindness to another person, or we do something for another person for no reward.** Compassion and kindness go hand in hand. Compassion does not always need to manifest itself in action; it is wonderful when it does, but it can simply be a kind thought directed towards another person.

Relearning to be kind

Unfortunately, most of us spend our lives seeing the world from a very, very narrow perspective. That perspective is ourselves. Children, when they're very young, are highly egocentric. Their world revolves around them. As time passes, most move into adulthood and leave the egocentricity of childhood behind, but others don't. The world is still all about them. How can the world serve me? What are people doing for *me*? And we see the world in terms of what it can give us. We should try to look at the world in terms of what we can give it. The one thing we can all do is care about the suffering of others, and do something about it. **Don't be a spoiled child, looking at the world in a self-oriented way.** When we see the world in terms of how it can help us, from an ego-based perspective, we become almost incapable of compassion because of our own selfish view of the world. We cannot see beyond our own need. We become needy and dependent.

There is an extraordinary truth that I have learned, which I didn't at first believe until I put it into practice. The lesson is: **you cannot help another person in this world without helping yourself as well**. That includes not only physical help but prayerful and positive thoughts directed towards another person. I know this works. My experience is that **when you demonstrate compassion to other people it comes back to you in different forms**. Whenever I find myself faced with a difficult person, no matter how rude, offhand or aggressive they are, I make a very conscious effort to be kind to them in thought and action.

Compassion is not about weakness, it is about strength and personal growth

In my heart I keep a feeling of compassion for this person. If they are angry, I am genuinely sorry for their anger. I find that when I have made a conscious effort to be compassionate in my thoughts and actions, almost every time their anger, hate, rudeness or mild aggression defuses almost in front of my eyes. **It is the ability to feel sympathetic towards another person that connects us to our own humanity.** I do my best to understand the sufferings of others, so when people are rude or aggressive I try to understand that they're in pain, they're having a bad day, or maybe they just don't like me.

Either way, how I respond to them is my responsibility and under my control, so I choose compassion. We all can choose compassion if we make the effort.

Your compassion touches other
people's hearts and souls in ways
you will never know.

Today

Look for opportunities to demonstrate
compassion to others in thought,
word and action.

Give to Receive

'The habit of giving only enhances the desire to give'

Walt Whitman, US poet, 1819–1892

I have found that what you give you get back with interest. You give out anger — you get back anger in another form. You give out unkindness and unkindness comes back to you in another form. **You give out love, compassion, help, assistance and they all come back to you multiplied.**

Today I want you to reflect on giving. It is natural in life to want stuff. Stuff that we think we need. **No matter how much we have, we usually want more.** We want a slightly bigger house or a bigger car, we want a slightly more expensive coat, we want a better, longer, more fabulous holiday. Once we get it we want even more in order to replace what fundamentally we don't have, in the belief that by having these things we will be fulfilled and happy, that life will make sense and we'll stop worrying about stuff. Many mystics and spiritual masters have renounced possessions, but we live in the real world, in real time, with real jobs and real physical and material needs, so I'm not suggesting we go and sit on a mountain top and renounce the material world.

Don't become possessed by material things

People so often believe they will find security by possessing things, and in turn become possessed by them. How many people have you met who you would describe as mean-spirited or selfish? My experience has generally been that people whom you describe as mean-spirited or self-ish are to some degree or another insecure. Because they look at the world from the perspec-tive of 'what's in it for me?' what they don't have they want, and the things they have plenty of they seem to want more of. So if you adopt the mind-set that you will share what you have and give of yourself, your time and sometimes your money, and free yourself from that neediness to possess and hoard, you will find it liberating.

> Life is transient. It is not permanent. You're not taking it with you no matter how rich you are, so when you can – share

Let me put it in another context. Do you prefer to receive a gift or give a gift? When I was young, I liked to get gifts. Christmas or birthdays couldn't come fast enough because I had learned that I was going to get something and it was going to be great for me. My parents and my friends would give me presents and look on in a way that demonstrated that they were delighted to see me receive something I enjoyed. As I've got older I've come to seek the joy of giving, which creates moments of pleasure for other people.

> You need to realise that until you
> change the way you see the
> world nothing changes

This challenge is about changing our self-awareness as well as moving towards our goals while becoming physically fitter and eating better. **By taking control of our lives, we will create our preferred future.** It is about transforming the way we see ourselves in the world around us. If you see the world from a selfish, self-centred point of view, you will become that insecure person who is always looking to get more out of life than you put in. So understand the simple truth that by giving to life we get more back.

The more we give the more we receive.

Today

Look for opportunities to give.

Coincidence

'There are no mistakes, no coincidences. All events are blessings given to us to learn from'

Anon

I don't believe in coincidence. **I don't think anything happens without there being a cause, and your influence on this cause will often be greater than you can imagine.**

There is a school of thought that believes that thoughts are things, that the whole universe is a manifestation of energy, and that the physical appearance of the things we can see is not as real as we imagine.

If you were to study matter, you would learn that scientists originally believed the smallest unit was the atom, and the atom was the building block of all matter. Then some research scientists discovered the atom itself was constructed by even smaller particles, which led to an increase in sub-atomic particle theory. Then they started to examine the sub-atomic particles and discovered there are particles that make those up. These are sub-sub-atomic particles, and so it goes on.

What the findings reveal is that nothing is exactly solid. The atoms are energy, vibrating at such a phenomenal pace that they give the appearance of being solid, and when they bind together it creates the physical world we see. So, it is easy to make the case that all matter is energy. From that it is not such a great leap of imagination to accept that all matter seen and unseen is made of energy. It is also easy to take this a little step further by thinking that when you have an idea or thought, that too is a source of energy. So for me it is not so far beyond the realms of possibility that when we think about things, we create and connect to this energy.

We've all experienced that moment when the phone rings, you answer and a person you were just thinking of says, 'Hello', to which we immediately say, 'I was just thinking of you.' Or a film that you were talking about with a friend appears on TV that night.

Your subconscious determines reality

When you set a clearly defined goal, your subconscious mind looks for the evidence and the opportunities to bring it into reality without your conscious attention. Which is why as you wander through a book store in an apparently random manner, though you are only able to focus on one title at a time, your eyes can almost take in the entire scene, and if there is a book or a title or a subject that is of particular interest to you and which you need to be aware of, your subconscious mind will collect this information and bring it to the attention of your conscious mind. Your conscious mind will walk up, pick up the book and go, 'Great, just what I was looking for.' You may consider it at the time to be a coincidence, but there is always a reason of which you have no conscious awareness.

I have learned that **when we focus our thoughts on a strongly visualised goal, we attract it into manifesting in our lives.** 'Be careful what you wish for' is a useful warning. When you powerfully visualise and with forceful intention 'see' your goal, you release energy into the universe. You don't need to understand it to allow it to work.

When coincidence happens I've learned not to be surprised; in fact, I've had so many events of such astronomical probability occur in my life that I'm now completely unfazed when things like this happen.

A random event or a manifest coincidence?

I once spent some time living in Los Angeles, in Venice Beach. I had been given the opportunity to become a writer for a television show in New York, and they wanted me to write some sample material. I sat down at my typewriter and wrote a piece called 'Reunion'. It was about five people meeting, having not seen each other for 15 years. About 30 minutes into writing this sketch I developed a craving for some cheese-cake and a coffee. I decided that I'd take the dog, Max, who lived in the house. Once we had crossed the road, I let Max off his lead and he ran towards the beach, down a narrow alley. As he got to the bottom of the boardwalk I saw two people some distance away.

At that exact moment I shouted after Max. The two people stopped about 20 yards away and one of them peered up the alleyway, and a familiar voice called out, 'Robin? Is that you?' It was a friend from Glasgow, who I hadn't seen for over seven years. He came back to the house and told me he was on a business trip to LA and was visiting Venice Beach Boardwalk because at the last minute a meeting he had been due to attend was cancelled. We had a reunion of our own.

Be open to coincidence when it occurs in your life and do not think of it as some random event. There is order in the universe, some of which we can see and can explain but much of which we cannot see and cannot explain. The important thing is to understand that it's real. Whether we believe in coincidence or not, it does not stop it influencing or having an effect on our lives.

Though it may not seem obvious
there is order in the universe.

Today

Be open to coincidence in your life.

Self-Limiting Beliefs

'The recipe for perpetual ignorance is be satisfied with your opinions and content with your knowledge'

Elbert Hubbard, US editor, 1856–1915

I actively hope that you are becoming increasingly aware of your ability to achieve more than you ever believed possible. You are changing your view of yourself from someone who held negative beliefs about your potential that restricted you. I call these 'self-limiting beliefs'. You are now changing your negative self-beliefs into positive ones. **Every time you achieve a goal that you have never achieved before, no matter how small, you deconstruct a previously held limiting belief.** Over the next four weeks you will be getting out of your comfort zone continually, and setting small goals that previously you have not been able to realise, simply because you thought you couldn't.

Dominant thoughts direct our actions

Today I want you to reflect on the self-limiting beliefs you hold to be true, which have no basis in reality. **We move in the direction of our dominant thought.** What we think about we manifest in our lives. It is you who has created your self-limiting beliefs and by focusing on them they have grown in your mind. From vague notions that maybe you are clumsy, shy or destined to be poor, you have constructed genuinely inhibiting beliefs that block your road to your success.

> Your subconscious mind does not know
> the difference between something that
> is real and something that is imagined.
> So what you think about appears real

The use of language becomes powerful and important. If you say, 'I can't', then your subconscious mind will take this information and believe it to be true. So if you say, 'I can't learn to speak a foreign language', your subconscious mind will take on board and make your self-image compatible with the belief that you indeed cannot learn to speak a foreign language. When you try to learn a foreign language the deep-seated subconscious view of yourself kicks in and will self-select information congruent with that belief.

> If you hold self-limiting beliefs,
> you limit your life until you
> deconstruct them

You need to identify whatever limiting beliefs you have. Many you've had for so long, you're not even aware that they're influencing your life.

One of the biggest self-limiting beliefs that I come

across, and I wonder if this sounds familiar to you — it's a big one — is quite simply this: 'I'm just not good enough', or 'I'm not worthy enough' to receive love, wealth or happiness. Hopefully as children we receive unconditional love and praise on a daily basis. But our parents or other carers may give out other messages and change the way we see ourselves by saying (usually unwittingly or without malice), 'No one's ever going to want to marry you', 'You'll never be happy', 'You'll never make money', 'You'll never get a good job', and so on, and these thoughtless remarks if repeated often enough can develop in our minds and become future self-limiting beliefs.

It is interesting to note that immigrants from third-world countries are four times more likely to become self-made millionaires when they emigrate to a first-world country, than the people who are born in the first-world country. One of the reasons is that, driven to survive and succeed, many of them put no limits on themselves or what may be possible. When they arrive in a new land all they can see are opportunities.

Deep in our minds we may all discover that we hold some silly beliefs about ourselves that have no basis in truth and are either based on the opinions of other people or on opinions we formed of ourselves in a moment of insecurity. But unfortunately we hold them to be true now, and because of that they become our vision of the future.

Change your views, change your expectations and you will change your future

Thought is the source of our lives and as long as we think negative, unhappy thoughts, we will see a negative, unhappy future. Examine today what self-limiting beliefs you may have and ask yourself: why do I believe this is true?

Let me give you a good thought for today. You are not stupid, ugly or destined to be an unhappy failure. I want you to examine any negative beliefs you may hold and quite simply abandon them or change them to positive beliefs.

Convert negative thoughts into positive ones

Do you want your children to grow up afraid of the dark? Believing they are incapable of creating success and happiness or finding the love of their life? Of course not! Do you want them growing up believing they are nobody special, they're not important, their opinion has no value to anyone? Of course not! You want the best for them – happiness, love, success and health. That is the least you would want for them. It is certainly the least you should want for yourself. Trust me, change your self-limiting beliefs and you open up a world of possibilities, which is why we must let go of negative thoughts about our potential and replace them with positive ones.

The limits you set upon yourself
define your world and your potential.

Today

Reflect upon what self-limiting beliefs
hold you back and change them.

Focus

'If I have ever made any valuable discoveries, it has been owing more to patient attention, than to any other talent'

Isaac Newton, English scientist, 1642–1727

I remember being asked to talk to a well-known actor and a friend of mine about motivation, as they were going on a long trip and wanted to get a better understanding of how to handle bad experiences. The actor gave me his total, 100% undivided attention, and it wasn't an act either. I've met very few people who when you speak to them give you their full undivided attention. Some people do it naturally and others have the ability to turn it on and off at will, and make the person they are speaking to feel as though they are the most important person in the world.

Whatever situation you are in today, I would like you to focus on *being* there completely. If you find yourself having a conversation with a colleague that you feel you've had many times before about a particular issue, instead of waiting for the conversation to end or interrupting them, this time pay attention, listen and give them your undivided attention. Focus entirely on what they are saying and then focus on your response.

Focus leads to the right actions

It is by using this ability to focus our attention on a specific point that we can maximise our ability to take the right and most effective action. How often are you introduced to someone and you're told their name and 10 seconds later you can't even remember it? Why? Because you're not being present in the moment and not focusing your attention where it's meant to be.

> To realise your goals you must keep your focus locked on to what you want

Sports people talk about this awareness of the 'present moment' when they are in 'the zone'. You look into the eyes of a high-performing sportsperson when they are performing at the top level of their ability and they seem to be in a trance. They are so focused on the one thing they have trained to achieve that they are oblivious to all else. Their attention is absolutely fixated on one point, one kick, one sprint, one leap, one moment in time. **Every second is a moment in time. Give your attention to the task in hand.**

This awareness of giving your attention to the present moment lies at the core of the philosophy behind the 42 days. Focused goals and focused efforts give focused results. Whoever you are with give them 100% of your attention. Listen, pay attention and be focused. Whatever you do with others or on your own, be 100% present in the moment.

The more you can focus your attention on the present situation the greater your opportunity to extract the maximum value from it

I think of focus as being a convergence of energy and attention. **Examine your level of focus in your life. Too often we think we are giving it our all, when in reality we are barely engaged.** Only you can change that situation.

Without focus we lose direction.

Today

Give 100% of your attention to every action you take and see the difference it makes, not only for yourself but for the people with whom you interact.

Acceptance

'Dare to be what you are,
and dare to resign with a good
grace all that you are not
and to believe in your own
individuality'

Henri-Frederic Amiel, Swiss poet, 1821–1888

Today I'd like to reflect upon the notion of acceptance. Many people go through life being unhappy and feeling discontented, especially with things over which they have no control. They get themselves bent out of shape by these events. They become angry, frustrated, give up on their dreams and their ambitions. **It is important to recognise the difference between those things we can control and those things over which we have no control.**

Accepting things doesn't mean that you are unwilling to challenge them and it doesn't mean you give up all hope. It means you put things into perspective.

Acceptance leads to respect

Many people are deluded enough to think they are perfect, and feel it is their right to sit in judgement of others. Make no mistake, all religions, all spiritual masters and many philosophers agree on this point: even though we may look different, we are all equal.

Historically, the democratic institutions of the world respect equality for all. It is a fundamental basis of every democratic society that everyone is equal. But I'll bet there is a prejudice you carry around. It may be subtle but all the same there are some people in this world you may feel superior to, and others whom you may feel inferior to.

To accept yourself as you are is simply to accept the reality of your present situation, and if you don't like it, you know what? You really can change it. Therefore **if we are to be accepting of ourselves, then it stands to reason, in fact it demands, that we are accepting of other people.** It requires that we are non-judgemental.

Never judge appearances

One Friday evening some 20 years ago I was going by train into central London to meet some friends. As I waited for a train I noticed a man standing some way from me. He was wearing black trousers with highly visible white socks, and black shoes that seemed too big for him. He had an imitation-leather jacket on, with an elasticated waist that really pinched around his back. He had the collar of his white shirt over the collar of his imitation-leather jacket, and a bad Elvis Presley haircut. I thought he looked ridiculous. I stood there looking at this fellow, thinking how silly he looked because he obviously thought he looked great.

Two people arrived at the station, recognised him and walked up to him, and they greeted each other warmly. They started to laugh and talk and were all pleased to see each other as they prepared for what I am sure was going to be a big night out for them. At that

---

moment I felt deeply ashamed of myself. I had no right to judge this man, I didn't know his life, I didn't know his situation. I had no right then or now to judge another person for the way they dress, and yet that is exactly what I had done. I had in my mind not only formed a strong negative opinion of another person, I had decided that his clothing was deeply uncool, and therefore he was somehow an idiot. Yet it was in that precise moment, when his friends greeted him and they were all laughing together, that his humanity returned. I saw a person, who, like me, wants to enjoy the company of friends, be loved and enjoy life. I realised that evening on the railway platform that in judging others we dehumanise them and reduce them to objects of subjective analysis. No matter how often we do it, the reason, I believe, is always the same. We do it to reassure ourselves that we are better than them, and we do that because we are insecure.

When we judge another, we rarely do it because we're right, we do it to make ourselves feel better

When you meet another person, you do not know the journey they have travelled, the traumas that have shaped their lives and the pain they have suffered. Acceptance is just that. Accepting without judgement ourselves and others, being unconditional in accepting them as they are and not as we *think* they should be.

I've learned that acceptance is not to be confused with indifference. We all have the power of free will. What we do with it is ultimately our choice. I abhor prejudice, bigotry, narrow-mindedness, cruelty, unkindness – all those characteristics. The fact that people hold beliefs, values and behaviours that I find negative and destructive does not mean that I feel I can sit in judgement of them. I may not understand or comprehend why they do what they do, but I've learned it is better to accept people as they are and seek to change them by my example, or other means.

By sitting in judgement of the world around you, you are not a participant, you are simply remaining an observer. To change the world you have to participate.

All spiritual masters and all great religions state that you must not be attached to things, in the form of possessions, or ego, in the form of self-importance. By being attached to our egos we stunt our ability to see clearly. When we cannot see clearly, we judge things incorrectly and for the wrong reasons. **We have to learn to accept ourselves and other people as they are.**

Accept people as they are, not as you would like them to be.

Today

Recognise the circumstances in your life over which you have no control – accept them as they are and move on.

Action

'Thinking is easy, acting is difficult, and to put one's thoughts into action is the most difficult thing in the world'

Johann Wolfgang von Goethe, German writer, scientist and philosopher, 1749–1832

You are now over a third of the way through the challenge. I hope it has captured your imagination and has helped you put real focus into your daily goals and aspirations.

The challenge is about reintroducing yourself to your true potential. Today as you look back over the past 16 days what are you most proud of? Giving yourself wonderful goals? Sticking to your plan? Or the fact that every day you've taken action and are now well on track to succeed?

Nothing happens until you take action. This obvious fact of life is missed by so many people. The main reason is that they think they have so much time. They procrastinate. Tomorrow, next week, next month, next year, the year after, and it never comes. So many people wake up one day and discover they are old. And their youthful dreams are gone for ever.

Have the courage to act

In my last book, *You Can Change Your Life Any Time You Want*, I said that most people need crisis in their life before they take the action to change, and that we should not wait for the crisis. We should have the courage to take the action we need to take, and not settle for second best.

I cannot tell you how many people I have met who have lost their jobs, been made redundant and later tell me they wish it had happened sooner, because they discovered that they really could fly when they flapped their arms, metaphorically speaking.

A major reason people fail to take action is that they are afraid they are going to fail. You know that if you don't take action you can't fail, because you didn't try — but you can't succeed either. This challenge is about enabling you to create for yourself the success you want. **Do not be afraid of failure, take action; if you fail then learn the lesson. If you don't try you'll never know.**

> When you fail, ask yourself two questions: what did it teach me and what will I do differently next time?

In life you can be a spectator or you can participate. We need to become major participants in the game of life. Every day you are taking action towards realising the goals, and changing the person you were into the person you want to be. No action is ever wasted. You either succeed or *you learn something*.

Excellence is no accident

A friend of mine has a classic 'six pack', the abdominal muscles that you tend only to see on first-class athletes. I once asked him his secret. He told me:

80 sit-ups every day. I met a fellow who played wonderful scratch golf. I asked him how he did it, and he told me: he hit 1000 balls a week throughout his teenage years and continues to practise most weeks. No real surprises there. It is as a result of taking positive and continual action that they are able to create the results they want. The same will be true for you.

We have to take action to get a result. No action you take will be wasted. Today, whatever actions you determine to take, feel good when you take them, appreciate the efforts you have made so far and recognise that these actions are stepping stones to success.

No action will give no result,
every time.

Today

Continue to recognise that every action
moves you closer or further away from
your goal, so always choose your
actions wisely.

Fear of Failure

'The way to develop
self-confidence is to do the
thing you fear and get a record
of successful experiences
behind you. Destiny is not a
matter of chance, it is a matter
of choice; it is not a thing to
be waited for, it is a thing
to be achieved'

William Jennings Bryan, US lawyer, politician, 1860–1925

Yesterday we looked at the concept of taking action. We've seen that the main reason that people don't take action is because they are afraid of failure.

A friend of mine has been successful in all the businesses he has created, and become a multi-millionaire in the process. He is a quiet, kind and intelligent man. While I was researching this book I asked him what is the key to success. He surprised me by declaring that he didn't have any specific philosophy. He reflected for a while then said, 'Failure is your first step to success.' I think there is immense wisdom in his view. **Failure is indeed your first step to success, because failure is our greatest teacher.**

As children, failure is something we seek to avoid. We seek praise, we want to be rewarded, we want to win, and if we don't win we can become very unreasonable. In many ways society has brought us up with the notion that winning is everything. Failure is a stigma to be avoided, and only winning matters. As a result many of us still beat ourselves up when we fail. Even when we fail in the simple daily tasks of our life, when we fail to stick to our diet or exercise or a course of study. We feel bad about ourselves and give up on our goals just a little bit more.

You can't fail if you don't try

The only value associated with failure in our lives is the value we give it. Remember you can overcome failure if you don't let your ego get in the way. It's easy to want to feel important and not want to damage that feeling by risking being ridiculed through failure. However, in my life, by not wanting to fail I simply didn't compete, and by not competing I was no longer a participant. I'd gone back to being a spectator. Don't be a spectator in life.

Failure will teach us lessons; success does not. Failure is never final – there is always something you can do.

At the end of your life, you will be able to live with your failures regardless of how many there are. But I promise you it is your regrets that will break your heart. It is the regrets for what might have been and never was. Often we hang on to our failures and remember them clearly with all the negative emotions that accompany them. We use them as a way of predicting our future.

Failure is no big deal. At the moment it happens it is painful. Yet as soon as we forget it and let it go it has no power over us.

Never think of or refer to yourself as a failure. It seriously damages your self-image at a subconscious level. **Failure is your teacher.** And although the lessons are painful, we will be destined to repeat them until we learn to learn from them. I have no doubt at all that I have failed many many more times than I have succeeded, and I will probably continue to do so. But it is my successes that I

145

choose to remember and dwell on and from my failures I learn the lesson then move on.

This challenge is about many things. It is about taking control of your life, changing the way you think about yourself and being honest with yourself. It is about learning to engage your mind and understand the impact of attitude on outcome. It is about being in control of your emotions, your day, your time, your feelings, your thoughts and your responses. **This challenge is about success and the success that will come to us through failure. It is not success without failure.** It is not going to be easy or instant. It will be transformational and life changing.

Today, I want you to think about your failures in a new light. Look back at your failures and see what you can learn from them, especially the big failures that still hurt when you think about them.

Win, lose or draw – it's a game

I played in a golf competition once against a fellow whom I didn't get on with. When he won he would gloat and arrogantly dismiss the match as not being much of a contest. If he lost he was insufferable, telling everyone that he had blown it, and thrown the match away. He couldn't be gracious in defeat.

In one competition we found ourselves in the final. We came to the second to last hole. We both put our second shots in the bunker. He took five shots to get out of it. I could have putted out of the back of the bunker, putted four more shots and won the hole, but I decided to play out of the bunker. My ball plugged in the face; four shots later it was still in the bunker. I lost the hole. I lost the match. I was physically stunned. I couldn't speak for an hour for fear that I would choke up. Even though people came up to me and said it didn't matter, all I could hear was this inner voice overwhelming me with a sense of failure.

I so desperately wanted to beat this fellow that I couldn't bear the concept of him beating me. That day I learned a painful lesson. It taught me not to have such a big ego, and it taught me to deal with things and accept a situation as it is and not to carry round regrets and anger. It made me realise, contrary to what some people believe, a game is only a game and though the result tastes sweeter in victory, it is not life and death — it is only a game. So I dropped my need to win at all costs and more importantly stopped defining myself by my results. As soon as I dropped the ego, all the emotions associated with it were dropped too.

Always put failure into perspective. See it as it is. Some failure can be very damaging to our lives and create tragedy. I don't want to minimise the importance of such events, but I do want you to learn the lessons and move on.

My mantra today is dare to fail. I dare you to fail. Failure you learn from, whereas regret will eat away at you. It doesn't matter if you fail, as long as you get up, dust yourself down and learn the lesson. People will admire you, respect you, and best of all you will admire and respect yourself.

Failure is never final unless
you accept it.

Today

In every failure you experience
learn the lesson and try again.

Don't Be Average – Be Great

'One machine can do the work of fifty ordinary men. No machine can do the work of one extraordinary man'

Elbert Hubbard, American editor, 1856–1915

As we move closer to the halfway stage of the 42-Day Challenge, I sincerely hope you are noticing changes in your life. Small or large it doesn't matter, as long as you are feeling more in control, developing a positive attitude, feeling physically healthier, enjoying exercise, seeing changes at work and in your self-image. You should be feeling more confident and more in control of life, and, significantly, have more of a sense of purpose in life. It just gets better from here on.

Today I want to look at the notion of living an above-average life. Of course, we should not think of ourselves as better or worse than anyone else, but we should recognise that we are unique individuals. Unique means special. It is good to **think of yourself as special**. No one exactly like you has ever lived before or shall pass this way again, so that's quite a burden of responsibility that has fallen upon your shoulders.

Corny as it sounds, until you learn to love and like yourself, it is difficult for you to truly love others. As soon as you love yourself irrespective of what you look like, sound like or dress like, the sooner you'll be open to the experiences of life in all their variety. **Loving yourself is not about vanity or egotism, it is about accepting yourself as a unique, special and capable person** with aspirations and ambitions, and feeling that you can achieve anything. You would regularly say to a child in your care that they could achieve whatever they put their mind to, and encourage and support their dreams and ambitions. Sadly we so often don't do this for ourselves.

Forget comparing yourself to others

Loving yourself is not about staring at yourself endlessly in the mirror telling yourself you're gorgeous. It is about accepting yourself and having a good sense of self-worth. So do not just relate to the status symbols you have in your life, such as your job or your car, rather relate to how you *feel* about yourself.

> Don't compare yourself to others – you don't know their life story

Never think of yourself as just being average. We should strive to be and think about ourselves as 'above average'. Though we logically may accept that we are unique and special, it is amazing how often we dismiss that thought and refer to ourselves as being ordinary. There is nothing wrong in being ordinary but I think that we should aspire to being extraordinary.

One of the primary causes of low self-esteem is that people tell themselves, 'I'm nobody special.' You are special. You should always seek to rise above the average. It is about pursuing your dreams and daring to be different. It is about marching to a different beat from others. Listen carefully for it, for that beat is the rhythm of your life.

Walk just a little faster

I knew a man who walked quickly everywhere all the time, and I asked him why. He told me he'd heard that the average person walked at around 2.8 miles an hour and he wanted to make sure he was faster than the average person. At the time he told me this I thought it was silly, but I see it was his way of trying to be above average.

For me average is like saying OK. How was your meal? 'It was average.' How was the film you saw last night? 'Average.' How is your life? 'Average.' I believe that you deserve better than 'average', you deserve GREAT.

Your life starts as a blank canvas. If you make a lot of brush strokes it becomes a very full canvas. It may be pretty, it may be an abstract; it doesn't matter what it is, the key is that you made the effort to make it real and make it happen. Make everything you do today and for the rest of your life above average when you can, and progress confidently towards the success you seek.

Why settle for average when you have greatness within you?

Today

Look at one aspect of your daily routine where you would most like to see great improvement and determine to make it happen.

Patience

'Adopt the pace of nature, her secret is patience'

Ralph Waldo Emerson, American writer, 1803–1882

We often seem to feel that success cannot come soon enough, and we are, for some reason, always looking at what we don't have instead of appreciating what we do have. The modern world is governed by time, and it is one commodity that we never seem to have enough of. **Though we certainly cannot control the passage of time, we can control how we experience it.**

Slow down

We shall today look at the options in situations where we would normally become frustrated or irritated, and make a conscious decision to let go of negative emotions. I have no doubt you have found yourself in the slow queue in a store or at an airline check-in desk. You may have waited a while to get to the front, when the person in front of you has a problem or an issue with the person serving them and a major delay ensues. We get angry more often than not. Rarely do we smile, shrug our shoulders and start reading a book, or have a good look around at our surroundings. We get angry, sometimes we feel victimised and think to ourselves, 'Why does this always happen to me?' In reality we chose to get angry and because it all happened so quickly we were not aware of it – in an instant we got bent out of shape and were hijacked by a negative emotional response, on a hair trigger. We need to slow down.

Patience requires practice, and
the more we practise the better
at it we become

Be the driver, not the passenger

When an event causes us to get upset and angry in
a heartbeat, we are, in effect, out of control, and are
going to end up where the anger takes us. Just like
a driver in a car is in control of the vehicle, we as
passengers will end up going where the driver takes
us. If we are driving the car, then we go where we
want. To stop yourself being hijacked by your
emotional response to every situation you have to
take control.

When I was a young lad I was advised to count
to 10 before speaking out in anger and to use that
time to reflect on what I was going to say and
what my intention in saying it would be. So if
someone hurt my feelings my instant emotional
response would be to hurt their feelings and say
something cruel and unkind. If I counted to 10,
however, that surge of anger would have diffused.
Without being aware I was being taught to practise patience.

Count to 10

Being patient keeps you from being emotionally hijacked and allows you to stay in control during a situation where you have little or no control. It is not easy at first but it is rewarding, because you reduce your stress levels, feel better about yourself and best of all remain in control of your feelings and responses to a situation.

Patience is an attitude

Earlier in the challenge we examined the phenomenal impact of attitude on outcome. There is an old saying: 'Your attitude and your aptitude determine your altitude.' As previously explained we have 100% control over our attitudes, so why not exert that choice?

Your attitude impacts on the way you think, the way you think impacts on the way you behave, the way you behave impacts on the way you perform and the way you perform impacts on what you achieve

Make the commitment to change your attitude for the better. To reflect a more positive outlook on life is the most important step we need to take. The transformation may be instant or it may not. The reason it may not be instant is that you may be in the grip of a lifelong negative pattern of behaviour, which you practise without thinking.

This is why **we have to practise until it becomes automatic**. So today when a situation arises where you would normally get frustrated and angry, make a determined effort to nip that feeling in the bud, and stay calm and in control. You may want simply and slowly to count to 10, or look at your surroundings to notice something you have never seen before, thereby distracting yourself away from anger and towards controlled calmness.

> ## So practise patience until it become automatic

You will find that the more you practise the easier it becomes. There is a wonderful quotation by Eleanor Roosevelt, who once said, 'No one can make you feel inferior without your consent', which is absolutely true. If you extrapolate that sentiment you arrive at a similar conclusion, which is: no situation or person can make you angry unless you choose to be.

Patience is like a muscle – the more you exercise it the stronger it gets.

Today

Begin to practise the art of personal patience.

Forgiveness

'To err is human,
to forgive divine'

Alexander Pope, poet, 1688–1744

As we arrive at the halfway point in the challenge, you will notice the difference in how you feel about yourself and the empowerment that is coming from taking positive action in your life.

Today I want you to reflect on forgiveness. Some people find it very hard to forgive those whom they believe have wronged them, and even harder to forgive themselves. As a result, they continue to carry the emotional baggage of the incident that upset them. Reliving the negative emotion, ranging from anger to fear and hate, doesn't do anyone any good at all. You can feed off it because in that anger you feel some kind of vindication or even victimisation. **So, what I'd like you to do today is reflect upon people or incidents that have happened in your own life – where you still feel aggrieved, and determine just to let it go. Forgive the person and yourself in your own heart.**

Imagine you were setting out to run a marathon. You've trained for six months, watched your diet, stuck to the schedule and are feeling pretty positive about the race. You've lost 26 pounds in weight over the six months through a wonderful regime of dedicated training and sticking to a very healthy eating plan. On the day of the marathon would you get 26 pounds in weight and strap it to your body and then try to run the marathon with the 26-pound weight on your back? I doubt it very much, and yet this seems to be what so many people do as they set out to achieve life change. At the moment of action they recall negative memories.

Forgive yourself to grow

The worst thing I find is when people beat themselves up about something they did long ago. You have to move on, because if you hang on to these destructive negative beliefs and emotions and do not forgive yourself, you will *not* be open to growth.

> Until you learn to forgive you will burden yourself with resentment

So, look back on actions you have taken of which you are not proud, such as hurting other people's feelings or damaging the reputation of another person through a careless act or a spiteful intention. I want you to reflect on these things and forgive yourself. I also want you to **forgive others who have wronged you.** There are people who have hurt you, have caused you pain and harm and have damaged you emotionally. These people may still be in your life and when you see them you feel resentment and anger. This emotion you hold within yourself is a terrible block to your wellbeing. Somewhere deep in your emotional memory you hold on to that resentment, to that shame, that sense of revenge. You hold on to the memory of that day; it is keenly felt and strongly remembered. Why won't you let it go?

I know people who hold on to an experience as

justification for why they are the way they are. They use it to try to make me understand why they dislike another person, telling me about this terrible tale of some injustice done to them, and they cling on to it for 20, 30, 40 years, often taking it to their grave. What did it gain them? Did it improve the quality of their life? Make them happier? I doubt it very much.

You can say sorry for the past

We've all done things that were stupid. We cannot recall them without feeling some degree of regret. We lock them away and throw away the key, but occasionally they pop into our mind, making us shudder. Because we are ashamed of what we did and we dislike ourselves for having done it.

In the absence of a time machine, here is what I want you to do. Tomorrow morning when you're into your visualisation exercise, I want you to recall that moment. When you reach the point of regret, freeze the image in your mind and clearly and with honesty say to yourself: 'I forgive myself for the hurt I caused, the shame I feel. I am not that person any more.' You may feel self-conscious but it will be very healing. It will release a negative block and you will immediately feel better about yourself. I promise.

Forgiveness is a fundamental part of almost every spiritual tradition

Not forgiving will create a block within you, and
will stop you from growing emotionally and spiritually. It is like a kink in a hosepipe. The water may
be able to flow in, but it doesn't flow out freely.

Our life may feel that it flows, but
until you remove the emotional and
spiritual blocks it will not flow freely
and the joy and fulfilment that should
be and are rightly yours are not
manifest in your life

For those who have seen loved ones suffer or die at
the hands of a drunk driver or a violent criminal,
forgiveness is very, very difficult, but not impossible.
Yet when people are able to forgive, from the depths
of such pain it allows them to begin to heal. Most of
us will never have such terrible experiences or painful
encounters, and won't need to let go of such terrible
pain. If such things were to happen to us I am sure
we would be well advised to seek the help of professional counselling to get through the pain, yet it
would be up to us — and us alone — to choose to forgive.

**Hold the idea of forgiveness close to your
heart today.** If there's one person you've felt angry
towards, call them today or write them a letter. Ask
those that you have harmed or caused pain to for

their forgiveness. Forgive yourself for getting angry, even at those little irritations that life throws at us — missing a train, a person in the queue taking longer than expected. Don't get angry, just forgive yourself for the feeling of irritation. Make forgiveness a habit, because it is a wonderful habit — through it you grow into a better person.

When you forgive, you grow and become a better person.

Today

Understand, appreciate and experience the power of forgiveness in your life and the lives of others.

Beliefs

'Live your beliefs and you can turn the world around'

Henry David Thoreau, American author,
poet, philosopher, 1817–1862

You are halfway through the 42-Day Challenge. Over the past three weeks I have reflected a number of times on the impact that our beliefs about ourselves and the world around us have on our lives.

Many beliefs are based on logic and reasoning that from personal experience we hold as correct. However, there are others that we were told were true, and we accepted them unquestioningly. We grew up thinking that everything we were told as children was and remains true. Discovering this is not the case can cause serious upset later in life.

I'm sure you have already seen the power of belief in the last three weeks, but once you firmly accept a belief as being real and true in your life it becomes real. Which is why **we need to review what it is we believe, about ourselves, our potential and the world around us.**

I hope that the challenge has given you an opportunity to re-examine and reassess what you now believe about yourself. I am sure your confidence has grown, your sense of purpose and your passion for your goals are strengthened. You are changing, due to the fact that you have changed your self-belief and your perception of your potential.

A powerful force

When we are young, we are (I hope) brought up with love, support and encouragement to believe that we can do anything we put our minds to. Yet it appears that by the age of 18 many young people have lost the childhood confidence they had; their beliefs have changed because people around them told them things about themselves that were simply not true, and, lacking confidence, they accept the other person's belief about them. One only has to look at the tragic consequences for people who suffer from anorexia. They believe they are over-weight, when the physical evidence of their anatomy is that they are at death's door. But the belief is so powerful that when they look in the mirror all they can see is fat. **Belief is very power-ful and we need to align it and make sure our beliefs about ourselves are good, positive and helpful in our lives.**

Examine your beliefs

Today review and reflect upon the beliefs you now hold and the beliefs you feel you may need to change to effect the success you seek. I suspect you're on track, I suspect there are very few nega-tive beliefs you still hold close to yourself, and if there are, examine them and slowly but surely through your visualisation exercise let them slowly fade away. **The positively held self-beliefs will enable the transformation you seek**, but they must be held close to your heart with great faith and a confidence that you will achieve your goals.

Face up to your fears

It is not what you say that will be an indicator of your personal beliefs, it will be what you do. We are not successful in life because of the things we say we're going to do; our success comes from what we achieve. But sometimes we don't want to challenge and change our beliefs because it will force us to face the things in life we fear.

> Consider your negative beliefs that have held you back, and let go of them

Believe you are smart, attractive, able and you can be successful in whatever way you desire – and you will act in accordance with that belief. Think of yourself as capable, special, unique, because you are. And don't put labels on yourself; liberate yourself with positive, powerful beliefs that will allow you to see yourself as a success now and in the future. Belief is the foundation of every major religious faith. What you believe determines what you can achieve.

Your beliefs will either limit you
or liberate you. You choose.

Today

Believe in yourself and the real-life
achievability of your goals.

Personal Commitment

'Whatever you can do or dream you can, begin it. Boldness has genius, power and magic in it. Begin it now'

Johann Wolfgang von Goethe, German writer, scientist, and philosopher, 1749–1832

Your successful completion of the 42-Day Challenge will not occur by chance, by good fortune or by luck. You have got here by the application of the single most important principle behind success: commitment.

There's a definition of commitment I like. Simply put it states, **'Commitment is doing the thing you said you will do long after your desire to do it has passed you by.'**

Do what you say you'll do

We're all familiar with enthusiasm. You probably began the 42 days with enthusiasm. Possibly, by the second or third day, the early morning starts or not being able to stick exactly to the healthy-eating plan put you under pressure that may have made you want to give up on the whole process, which is natural enough; in fact, it is the reason why people do give up. So unless you have the commitment to do exactly what you said you will do, you will fail.

Commitment is a strength. It is like a muscle in our body: if we use it regularly we strengthen it, if we don't it wastes away

Persistence pays off

You need to focus clearly on what you want to achieve, create a plan, have a very positive mindset and be committed to seeing through all the steps of the plan and **never, never give up.** Commitment can also be thought of in terms of persistence. Persistence is the all-important ability just to keep going no matter how often you fall down, no matter how despondent you may get. It is the ability just to get up and continue to try time and time again.

Don't get trapped in your false safety zone

All too often we stay in our comfort zone and talk about what we *want* to do, because that is the easy option. It's safe, there are no risks and we can always come up with 101 reasons why the time is not quite right for us to move, to take the new job, to emigrate, to start our own business. We can always find a reason if we don't really have the confidence to take action.

> To get out of our comfort zone takes commitment to our purpose

Commitment is not a skill. You don't go to school and learn it, you don't go to night classes to acquire it, and you don't go on courses to understand it. When I look back at the historical figures who have impressed me, time and time again they demonstrated the quality of endurance. They endured hardship, poverty, ridicule, to win through to reach their goals. I am very moved by the lives of the early explorers, who with only faith, hope and rudimentary equipment held to a fierce commitment to explore the world, to climb new mountains and challenge conventional thinking and create scientific breakthroughs.

Few of us become explorers but we can always discover something new about ourselves, about our friends and about our immediate world. You have to dig deep within yourself and find the commitment in your heart to follow through.

The fact that you are over halfway through the 42 days proves you have commitment. You will see the power that it has when you apply it in other areas of your life. **Reviewing your goals every day will powerfully reinforce them in your subconscious mind and your commitment will become automatic.** When you repeat an action often enough it becomes automatic: it becomes a habit. Something you do without thinking. We need to make into habits all the positive changes that we know will improve our lives. **To break bad habits requires a commitment to getting out of your comfort zone and forming new habits for your lifetime.**

Most people don't fail – they quit.
They give up on their dreams and
blame fate, bad luck, in fact anyone
but themselves. Too late they
realise they gave up too soon

Every person you meet who has succeeded in life will tell you a story of commitment and endurance, of pain but also of joy and satisfaction. **With less than 500 hours to go before you complete the challenge, continue to draw on the goals you seek to achieve by focusing your attitude, your purpose and your commitment to the tasks in hand, to create the success you want, through the next 19 days.**

You can do it.

Commitment is like a muscle: the more you use it the stronger it gets.

Today

Renew your commitment to your goals and your future success.

Smile

'Every time you smile at
someone, it is an action of
love, a gift to that person,
a beautiful thing'

Mother Teresa, nun and missionary, 1910–1997

How often in the course of a day do you smile? I think smiling is a wonderful thing to do. It is disarming, it puts people at their ease and it makes you feel good. Anatomists say that we use fewer muscles to smile than we do to frown. Also, when we smile the muscle memory of the facial expression connects to our emotional centres and makes us feel better.

Guillaume Duchenne was a French neurologist who studied the human smile and concluded that there are two smiles. One is artificial, the type you see when politicians are being photographed with young babies, or on models who are having to look happy for the advert they are appearing in. The other smile that Duchenne recognised is the joyful smile, the smile that uses muscles around the eyes, which you cannot use through direct instruction. This means you are using muscles in your face over which you have no motor control. The Duchenne smile comes from the heart.

When you smile, always smile from the heart

When I have been feeling particularly anxious, I force myself to smile. The reason is the muscle memory of faking a smile will actually fool the brain into registering feelings of happiness. OK, I'll happily admit that it is artificial, but by putting my facial muscles into the position they take when I smile I trigger some of the associated physical feelings that I remember from past memories of being happy, and as a result I feel myself relax.

Share a smile today

In today's busy and hectic society, especially in urban environments, we avoid eye contact with other people. We read stories of people who have been attacked in the street for the simplest of reasons, for looking at someone the wrong way. Yet travelling in many Asian countries I just love how freely people smile. In Thailand people smile all the time; it is disarming and very welcoming.

Smiling is good for you. It makes you feel good about yourself, it makes people feel welcomed. Whoever you meet today, give them a big smile. I do this as often as I can because I am connecting with them on a personal level.

Smile and mean it

I think a smile only really works when it is sent with love and positive intention from our hearts to make the other person know that we wish them well.

Smiling is a wonderful quality. When we see a baby, we automatically look into the baby's eyes to engage it and we give it a big silly sloppy smile. Our reward is when the baby mirrors our expression and smiles happily back. It is instinctive and natural that we smile. When we see a friend or loved one, or someone at a party who we'd like to talk to, we automatically smile. It is universal. I have never been anywhere in the world where a smile was not recognised, and appreciated.

Your smile must come with loving intention

Seek opportunities today to connect with other people in a spirit of friendship and joy. As you meet friends, colleagues or even strangers make a conscious effort to connect and smile.

The 42-Day Challenge is all about growth, personal transformation and success. It's about creating the new you. So today look for every opportunity you can to smile. Make an big effort to smile – you're over halfway through the 42 days, you're on the home straight. Celebrate the fact that you are having a positive effect on your life, and with as many people as you can today have a positive effect on their lives too.

Always to smile from your heart.

Today

Make a conscious effort to smile
and connect with others.

Kindness

'A tree is known by its fruit; a man by his deeds. A good deed is never lost; he who sows courtesy reaps friendship, and he who plants kindness gathers love'

Saint Basil, Bishop of Caesarea, 329–379

Be kind to yourself. We are often highly critical of ourselves. We don't recognise or reward ourselves for what we have accomplished. **Kindness asks very little of us other than a good intention in our hearts, which we put into our words and actions towards both other people and ourselves.**

Many people will suggest that being kind to yourself is weakness or selfishness. There's a difference between being kind to yourself and being self-indulgent. Being kind to yourself is to be considerate and think well of who you are and, if something goes wrong, not give yourself negative self-talk and feel bad about yourself.

Kindness is a strength of character not a weakness

Yet it can be revealing when we look at kindness in isolation that some people perceive it as a strength, others a weakness. I have no doubt that kindness is a strength of character and spirit. The more we exercise this wonderful virtue, the more we impact positively on those around us and the more good we create in the world. What you give in life you get back with interest. If you give kindness to the world and to those around you, it will be returned in many different ways.

U-turn in thinking

I have been at the receiving end of some extraordinary acts of kindness from friends and strangers too. When I was a student I was hitchhiking about 150 miles from New York with a friend. We had to catch our flight home two days later. We were stuck in a small rural part of New York State, miles from the freeway, with little traffic on the road. A pick-up truck drove by then returned, before doing a U-turn. The driver stopped and asked, 'Where are you guys going?' 'New York,' we said. 'Cool, throw your things in the back,' he replied. We threw our bags in the back and got in. He said, 'I saw you guys standing there, and I thought to myself, "Pick up those fellows and take them where they're going."' Now, at that point I wasn't sure if the man was a lunatic. 'We're going to New York, which I think is a little further than you would have planned,' I said. To which he replied, 'I'm not doing anything else today and I haven't been to New York in years.' He drove us all the way to New York downtown, delighted to have had the opportunity to do so. He refused offers of money for petrol. He just wanted to help us.

I'm sure you've received kindnesses you may have overlooked. Does there need to be a motive? People act with kindness and consideration because they want to help another person, and for many other personal reasons as well. Knowing that you've positively touched the life of another person by doing something selflessly is reward in itself.

Today I'd like you to reflect upon this one question. **What kind of person do you want to become – someone who is known for being tough, ruthless, a high achiever, or somebody who is known for being kind, positive, accessible and successful?**

Don't give away your soul

I believe that when we give up on the finer qualities of kindness, compassion and understanding, we give away a part of our soul. The cost is never worth the reward. If you have to give away your humanity to achieve your success, you've given away the most valuable part of who you are. I know business folk who are rich, powerful and revel in their reputation of being ruthless and tough. Their personal success is superficial and without meaning.

The 42-Day Challenge is about wholeness of body, mind and spirit. And **kindness is about your spirit. It comes from within**, it is a quality that I would ask you to nurture and develop. If your success comes at the expense of your humanity and inherent goodness, it will be hollow. You may appear to have it all, but in reality you'll have very little of any consequence.

Practise kindness until it becomes automatic

A kind thought on its own is good. **A kind action is priceless and you never know the value or the goodness it creates in the lives of other people.** It is never forgotten. It makes the person who receives it feel valued and it changes their life, if only in a small way, to have positive expectations of others.

Today when you perform your act of unconditional kindness go the extra yard and do something really special.

Have a nice day – really

One Sunday morning I had breakfast in a French café in London. I got talking to a teacher from a small town in America. She was visiting London alone. Her husband and children had surprised her on her birthday by buying her a round-trip ticket to London for seven days. We talked about the sites she had visited, and I gave her some advice regarding other places she would enjoy. As I was about to pay I discovered the waiter had inadvertently included her costs with mine. At the time I was living on a very tight budget – my

---

Sunday morning breakfast in the French café was the treat of the week. I didn't have a lot of spare cash, but it didn't cross my mind that I shouldn't pay for this woman. So I did. As I got up to leave I said goodbye to the teacher, wishing her a happy day and mentioning I'd taken care of her breakfast. I can vividly remember her look of surprise and gratitude to this day.

Don't allow others to dictate your compassion

I cannot see into the lives of people I meet, I don't know what hardships they have faced or what anxieties burden them. Yet in our day-to-day life we encounter people who are unreasonable, unhelpful and downright rude. Now, challenging as it may seem, these are the very people who need the most kindness. I am not suggesting that we condone rudeness or hostility, rather we do not allow ourselves to be affected by it. **Our capacity to think, feel and act in a spirit of kindness can transform anger into peace**, and all our positive emotions and the actions that we perform from a spirit of kindness help us grow into better human beings.

Kindness transforms both the
giver and the receiver.

Today

Be kind to yourself and others.

Unconditional Love

'In dreams and in love there are no impossibilities'

Janos Arany, Hungarian poet, 1817–1882

Mother Teresa, the Albanian nun who founded the Missionaries of Charity, a worldwide charity that provides palliative care for the sick and dying in the poorest parts of the world, summarized her philosophy in four words, 'Love all. Serve all', to explain the work that she and her community had undertaken.

As we move forward, today I would like briefly to reflect upon unconditional love. It follows on from kindness, but in reality kindness is bound to unconditional love.

The single most important relationship you ever have in your life is with yourself. Yet there are people who are severely handicapped by the very fact that they hate themselves. They don't like the way they look, behave or relate to the world and they do nothing about it. If you were to talk to them about the notion of loving themselves they would look at you blankly.

> Until you learn to love yourself as you are then you will only see your faults

Unconditional love is universal

The theme of unconditional love is very powerful throughout diverse philosophies and religions. Respect, compassion, trust, devotion, faith, prayer — they all find their origins in unconditional love.

Love is what we remember

The most successful people that I have met have this one thing in common: they all have pursued something they really love. They love their participation and the difference that it makes in their lives and to others. **Love what you do and do what you love is a recurring theme of success.** Your actions should be taken from a position of love.

Unconditional love is the single most dynamic influence. Think of it like this: there is love and there is hate. They cannot co-exist. You cannot be a hateful person and a loving person. It is one or the other. Love and fear cannot co-exist.

When we come to the end of our lives and we look back at the moments that made the difference, you will find that love was a large component. Your first day at school, your first kiss, the birth of a child, when you met your partner, when you got married, when you had children, when somebody died: these events will always involve an emotion where love is part of the dynamic. It is when we let go of our sense of personal ego and open up to unconditional love that we discover our true selves.

I read an article written by a man who had spent many years working with elderly people at the point of their life when they were close to death. He said that a recurring theme of the greatest obstacle people had found in their lives was the fear that their love would not be returned.

He went on to say that when they got through that barrier they learned that the feeling they sought in life was found in giving love, not in receiving it. True love comes from within us; it comes from our spirit and our heart. It must lie at the source of our actions and is found in our thoughts, our feelings and our intentions.

What you put into life, life gives you back with interest. Give anger, hate and spite, and they will come back and bite you. Give compassion, kindness and love, and they too will come back and comfort you

Love has no limits

I came across an article about a 12-year-old German boy who at the very end of the Second World War was personally presented with the highest military decoration – the Iron Cross – by Adolf Hitler, just as Berlin was being surrounded by the Allies. He had been awarded it for outstanding personal bravery in the service of his country. In his small town many miles from Berlin, the Russians were battling for control. As the battle progressed, he noticed eight German soldiers wounded and trapped by Russian fire. He jumped on a horse and he rode forward and in two journeys he brought them all back. He then found four more soldiers in a similar situation — isolated and in danger of being shot. Once again he rode to their rescue.

In total he rescued twelve German soldiers and in doing so had put himself in grave danger. He said, 'I got the soldiers away from enemy fire out of a sense of duty to my fellow man, I didn't do it for Hitler. I would have saved Russians or Poles in a similar situation.'

It's up to you

Understand that the more we can expose ourselves to the experience of both giving and receiving unconditional love, the better. We grow spiritually and emotionally. **We can make a huge difference to how we feel about ourselves and how the world feels about us.**

If it isn't unconditional love then
it isn't love at all.

Today

Reflect on the love in your life
that is in reality conditional, and
make a commitment to change it.

Trust Your Intuition

'We heed no instincts
but our own'

Jean de La Fontaine, French writer, 1621–1695

You may have become aware over the past few weeks that your confidence is growing and your decision-making ability is becoming more precise. You are learning to trust your gut instinct as you have been developing your powers of intuition.

I don't consider intuition as anything especially mystical or spooky. We all have the power of intuitive reasoning. In fact, **I believe intuition is instinctively knowing something without going through a rational process to arrive at that point**. It may be just an impression that something is, without having any firm evidence for it, a manifestation of our subconscious mind.

For me it's not a big step of the imagination to believe that we're able to process information so quickly that it appears in our conscious mind apparently without any thought.

People talk about visiting a place and falling in love with it right away. Looking to move homes they visit countless properties until they walk into the one they know is 'home'. People talk about love at first sight, meeting a person and intuitively knowing that this is the person that they are 'meant' to be with, their soul mate.

On a more mundane level, have you ever gone into a store and instantly seen a sweater that you just had to have? It's exactly what you were looking for and you just found it there and in a heartbeat you went, 'That's it.' How did you know so quickly? Finding the sweater in the store was not such a difficult thing to do; I believe that in your subconscious mind you know the colours you like, the styles you like, and when you walk into the store your brain is able to take in the whole picture and almost focus in on that sweater without you being aware you have seen it – your brain immediately draws your attention to the sweater. You see it and suddenly there's a sense of knowing 'that's the one I've been looking for'.

Why do we fall in love with a place that we have never been to before? Maybe in our subconscious minds it existed before – a déjà vu experience – or maybe there is an ambience, a mood, a feeling, a presence about this place that makes you very calm. Falling in love at first sight, you meet another person and just sense their energy, sense their spirit and for reasons that sometimes just go beyond any understanding you instantly fall in love.

> Every experience you have in your life is also experienced and stored emotionally in your mind

Recognising the signs

I grew up in Glasgow at a time when there was much random violence, frequently due to the influence of alcohol, and gangs of youths with nothing to do would roam the streets venting their anger on each other, on other gangs and, sometimes, innocent members of the public. The newspapers were full of stories of people who had been stabbed, badly beaten or killed through violent assaults.

I learned very quickly to recognise potential trouble. To recognise people with an aggressive spirit, who may have had a smile on their face, but whose eyes told a different story. I learned to read eyes, to read body language, to read mood, intention, speech patterns, even right down to the way people dressed and moved in a bar. I did this unconsciously, but it saved me many times from getting myself into violent situations.

Follow your instincts

I've intuitively at times in my life left my house for a flight much earlier than I needed to, only to discover there was a major traffic jam and had I left later I wouldn't have made it. I don't consider this to be coincidence; I believe I'm in tune with what is going on around me at such subtle levels, though I'm rarely conscious of it.

I can walk into a bar or down a street anywhere in the world and know if it is safe or not. I trust my instincts; I trust my intuition. Today I want you to do the same. **For the next few days, trust your instincts when it comes to making decisions.** The first response, your first gut feeling in any scenario is almost always or certainly often the right one.

I trust my first gut instinct. Yes, I get it wrong sometimes, because I think more than I need to or

I've over-analysed a situation. I'm not claiming it's 100% correct all the time, but the more you are aware of it, the better it gets. **I've found that when I've overruled my instincts it has been to my cost.** I should have listened to my first intuitive feeling.

There is much we do not understand, and therefore we dismiss or ignore. Don't ignore and certainly don't dismiss your intuitive powers. **People who are goal-oriented experience more coincidence, spot more opportunities and are able to react to opportunities when they do occur because they are intuitively sensing the opportunities and the actions they need to take.** Sometimes we get a gut feeling and sometimes we don't. When you do, learn to trust it.

Be aware of the moments where
you feel your intuition is trying to
tell you something, then listen.

Today

Always be open to your intuition.

Celebrate

'Celebrate every success no matter how small it may be because when you do, you grow'

Anon

In my earlier book *Natural Born Winners* I identified seven principles that are common to creating success. The seventh of the principles was celebration. The rationalisation was that when we celebrate a success, no matter how small, what we do is positively reinforce our self-image as being one of success.

By positively celebrating an event, from a small pat on the back and 'well done' to full-blown party and carnival, we are creating a stronger, more positive self-image of ourselves as a successful achiever. So when we go into another situation, we subconsciously draw on the memory of success, which has been powerfully embedded in our mind.

Today, do something that celebrates your success so far. We can celebrate success every day of our life in simple small actions. **Don't think of the simple achievements in your life as being unimportant. Every success is important.**

When you look back in life there will be many moments that you can recall vividly. Among them, celebrations will stand out: birthdays, weddings and anniversaries. Obvious moments where we recall a celebration. The memory of the celebration is still keenly felt and the emotions experienced at the time are also recalled. How often have you heard a funny story you know you have heard many times before about a shared mishap you experienced with a friend many years before, and retelling the story makes you laugh long and hard every time? The emotional memory is being reactivated. This is why it is important in our day-to-day lives that we create small memories of success and achievement through celebrating our success no matter how small.

> The more you can find to celebrate and feel good about, the better

You don't need permission to jump for joy

Like children we want to be accepted. We want to fit in. And nothing makes us happier than being told we're going to a party. Even if it's the smallest party in the world with just your parents and you sitting at a table eating cake. Instinctively, we like the feeling that celebrating brings us. Yet as grown independent, free-thinking adults we don't think to celebrate unless there is a formal occasion to be acknowledged. I think we should put the act of celebration into perspective. I believe **celebration can take many forms, from simple words of encouragement and small actions to big parties – they all impact on us in a positive and enjoyable way**.

You don't have to wait until it's your birthday or someone else's birthday, or Christmas or Easter or an anniversary for an excuse to celebrate. In fact, every day you're alive is a reason to celebrate, and

I don't say that lightly. I think too often we take so much for granted in our lives: our health, our prosperity, our friends, our family. I think acts of kindness and love are good examples of what I mean by small celebrations.

> When we consciously decide we should celebrate we actively build up and strengthen our self-image

Doing the things we enjoy and sharing them with the people whose company we enjoy is time well spent, so be sure to make time to do so in your life. Reflect on looking for opportunities to celebrate success and share in the celebrations of others.

Celebration reinforces our self-image in a very positive way, and makes us feel good about who we are and what we have achieved.

Today

Celebrate your progress so far, by doing something you enjoy.

Time to Lighten Up

'If there is light in the soul, there will be beauty in the person. If there is beauty in the person, there will be harmony in the house. If there is harmony in the house, there will be order in the nation. If there is order in the nation, there will be peace in the world'

Chinese proverb

You have now reached the five-week mark – an entire month. A twelfth of your year devoted to transforming yourself, creating new habits of success and recognising your true worth, an exciting period of self-discovery. It's well worth it, for you and your family, friends and colleagues, and the world at large.

You have undoubtedly put in hard work, honest analysis and faced some serious home truths in getting this far. But **this is not a competition or a formal exam. There's no panel of judges waiting to give you marks for your performance along the way.**

A day without laughter is a day wasted

Laughter is good for you

Science has proven something that I think we've all always known, and that is that laughter is good for you. It reduces the blood pressure, it lowers our heart rate, it releases marvellous mood-enhancing endorphins into our bloodstream. If you can't have a laugh, you miss the opportunity to fully experience the world. There is nothing better than joyful, exuberant, spontaneous laughter, especially when it is shared. We should look for opportunities to find laughter and to share it in our lives.

We can in life meet people who embody unpleas-
ant characteristics: arrogance, conceit, self-importance,
prejudice and a condescending manner. They take
themselves very seriously indeed, which makes me
realise that I would never want to be like that. The
best way I can think of to avoid it is just *don't take
yourself too seriously* and, generally speaking, we should
as an American friend of mine used to say, 'lighten
up'. People who take themselves very seriously
generally have big egos and tend to be insecure.

> Don't be attached to all the things
> around you, and don't be attached
> to your ego

Leave your ego behind

As they grow up most people go through a period
of insecurity where they feel the need to be
respected, admired and important. It is no doubt a
part of our adolescent development, as we go from
childhood into early adulthood. We want to be
taken seriously and we want to be admired by our
friends, respected by our peers. We want to be attractive to the opposite sex, so we don't really laugh at
ourselves. I have no doubt I was like that during my
teenage years.

Our worth is not found in our self-importance, it is found in our self-esteem

Most of those completely fulfilled and happy people I have met throughout my life had this one thing in common: they did not have outsize egos or impose a sense of their own self-importance on other people.

Your unchecked ego has a big appetite

Your ego, if you start to identify with it, becomes a terrible beast and it's got a voracious appetite. It needs a lot of feeding, and you just have to look at the excesses of some of the biggest egos of the world to realise the truth of that. The way to overcome your ego is not to feed it, but to starve it. How do you starve it? Serve others. Laugh freely, at yourself. Listen to others with interest and be happy and pleased in their successes.

There are many ways to overcome the needs of the ego if we simply take our focus away from ourselves and our own sense of importance. Genuinely practise the art of being patient, the art of kindness, compassion; serving others is the fastest way to getting away from a sense of self-importance.

Be your own person

Don't be a people-pleaser simply so they like you. It doesn't matter what they think, the only thing that matters is what *you* think. What do you think of yourself? If you think you're very important and people should show you respect, then alarm bells need to go off. If your sense of yourself is defined by what others think, say and feel about you, you are taking yourself too seriously, and making your happiness conditional.

> You're here for a good time, not a long time, be sure you have a good time

The 42-Day Challenge is about renewal, self-discovery and succeeding in your life goals, big and small. It is about growing physically, mentally and spiritually. It is about becoming a complete person, reconnecting with your sense of ability to achieve the goals you set yourself and being happy. Life is here to be enjoyed, not endured. So go with the flow, don't worry and be happy. Find opportunities to laugh, watch happy films and read funny books. Go and listen to comedians in a club, it has the most healing qualities about it. **Laughter is the most wonderful feeling, it takes us away from all our worries and all our concerns.**

219

Don't go looking for the approval of others or be concerned about the opinions they may have about you. You know who you are, so don't think of it as a big deal, be humble, and lighten up.

Don't worry about being important,
or seeking the approval of others
because your ego demands it.
Be yourself and laugh more.

Today

Enjoy life and don't always
take yourself too seriously.

Determination

'A failure establishes only this,
that our determination to
succeed was not strong
enough'

John Christian Bovee, writer, 1820–1904

One of the key benefits of the six weeks is that it acts as a detox. Among the seven rules of the 42 days is no alcohol. Initially many people can't think what the point of this denial is all about. The purpose is to get you to develop and utilise your willpower to determine a course of action.

Your willpower becomes stronger when you exercise it

You have to resist temptation to create new habits

How often when you are giving up alcohol, cigarettes, unhealthy foodstuffs or making some other lifestyle change does someone come along and offer you the one thing you have sworn to give up? They tell you, 'Well, one cigarette is not going to spoil your success' or 'Not going to the gym as you planned, that's not the end of the world.' They're right, it's not the end of the world – but it's not sticking to our plan either. We're being weak, we're letting ourselves down and in so doing we damage our self-image just a little bit. No matter how much we justify it, we wish we hadn't done it. I have no problem saying no, because my focus is always on my goal, and I only have to imagine how I will feel if I give in to enable me to keep my determination levels high. Right now you're looking forward to completing the challenge and not letting yourself down. So determine not to give in.

> Letting ourselves down is one of the easiest things to do. Unless we determine that come what may we will just not give in

In the course of the 42 days, you will have had a number of opportunities presented to you to cheat or give yourself a day off the challenge. Whether you gave in or not was up to you. If you did, it is no big deal, as long as you don't repeat the error.

Now as you are well on your way to completing the 42 days, understand the power of determination. I would ask you to keep that sense of determination in everything you do – **when you say you are going to do something, do it**. You can fool other people, but you can't fool yourself. Even though you may justify your actions, you will know that you've let yourself down.

If you don't determine to make something happen it won't happen. Wanting it to happen, wishing or hoping for it doesn't make it happen, you have to determine to make it happen

Most of us will have experienced more failure than success in our past. This challenge is about putting our life on track and reconnecting us with our ability to succeed. **By realising the purpose behind your goals it is easy to become committed, motivated and determined.** Focus on the positive benefits that succeeding in your goal will give you. You must make a determined commitment to stick to the journey no matter what discomfort or pain you may experience; difficult emotions and memories will pass. **Nothing stays in a state of permanence apart from love. Everything else disappears.**

Your ability to determine doesn't come from a bottle, or a three-day residential course; it comes from within. It's not a skill, it is another attitude that we have 100% control over.

As you go through the rest of the 42 days you will notice the steps you need to take becoming automatic. Indeed I'm sure a lot of it has already become routine.

Quietly and with confidence tell yourself every day, 'through my actions and determination I shall succeed', and you will.

Today

Reflect on the power of determination in your life.

Death

'Life and death issues don't come along that often, thank God, so don't treat everything like it's life or death. Go easier'

Thomas Arnold, British educator, historian, 1795–1842

Woody Allen once summed up death very succinctly when he said, 'It's not that I'm afraid to die, I just don't want to be there when it happens.' We think, or, more accurately, we *don't* think about death very often because it's not a particularly happy thought. It's not something we actively look forward to.

The human mind cannot conceive of not existing. The ego of the mind views death abhorrently, and will do everything in its power to avoid that moment in time when it ceases to exist. Past emotional memories we associate with death will cause us discomfort and even emotional distress, so it is quite natural that this is a topic we don't dwell upon very often.

This reflection is not about dwelling on physical death, and it is certainly not intended to be gloomy – quite the opposite. It is about learning to be fully alive in the present moment, about following your dream; it's about taking chances. It's about living.

Choosing courage over fear

When I was 29 I was in hospital being treated for cancer and during this time I thought about dying and in particular about my funeral. It was fast turning into a major Hollywood production as I lay in my hospital bed. I tried to imagine what people would say about me, what kind of person I would be remembered as, but more than anything else I thought about my regrets. As a result of that experience, I decided not to focus on or worry about death but to concentrate entirely on life, and live in the present moment and seek to do the things that I knew would bring me joy.

> When you concentrate your time and attention in the present moment, the fear of death disappears

The opposite of fear is not courage; the opposite of fear is love. We're not alive because we are cheating death, we're alive because we're living life to its fullest. So be sure to live by focusing your attention on the here and now. Make sure that as you progress through life you achieve the experiences that you want, by not postponing them endlessly.

Stop worrying and start living

Focus on doing the many significant things you want to do in life. The people who spend their lives being afraid or worrying about the future never open up to the possibility of living today. They are afraid to fall in love in case their hearts get broken, they're afraid to take chances in case things go wrong. Because they fear love, they don't take the chance, they don't reach out, their egos are very sensitive.

Their lives become collections of missed opportunities and regrets.

My view is that you have this physical experience called life, but there is also a spiritual experience that very few people ever get a glimpse of. You have a soul that it is your essence. It has always been, it always will be. **You are a spiritual being having an earthly experience in which birth and death are simply points on the time continuum.**

I want you to think about all the things you want to see and all the things you want to do in your life. If you want to, make a list – it can be as big as you want. It should be balanced between giving, receiving, experiencing and growing. It should not simply be about accumulation. These experiences should be meaningful to you and you should determine to do them, because if you don't you'll only regret what might have been.

> Our lives are not measured by what we make, rather they are measured by what we become

Make sure that in your life you become fulfilled and significant. Our lives are not about who has got the biggest car or the most money. I have come to the realisation that our lives are about experiencing life and love in all its fullness.

A lesson from the elderly

Studies with elderly people and those who work with the dying reveal much about meaning and purpose in life. With the following short reflections to give you food for thought, I want to stimulate your thinking. I want to leave you with some of the reflections and ideas that the researchers have written about, and the common themes that emerged from those many conversations.

Comments from the elderly reflecting on what life has taught them

Love is timeless and real.
When we face our fears, our fears disappear, when we think about our fears they grow.
Life is about being, not only doing.
We cannot change other people but we can change ourselves.
You should do what you love.
We should not make happiness conditional.
God does not see the limits that we put on ourselves.
Forgiveness means letting go.
Fear is no match for love.
Now is the only moment we have, so live it to the full.

We should play and have fun, you're here for a good time, not a long time.

Refusing to accept situations we cannot change exhausts us, and saps us of our power.

You can't change the past but you can choose a good life and peace of mind for the future.

We have all we need to be happy.

There is no problem or situation that God cannot deal with, and the same is true for us.

All positive emotions come from love and all negative emotions come from fear

There's a lot to reflect on there. If any one of those beliefs has any resonance for you, carry it around in your heart today.

You will leave your mark on the world by the way you lived your life not your death.

Today

Determine to live every moment to the full, and leave your mark.

Your Health

'To keep the body in good health is a duty . . . otherwise we shall not be able to keep our mind strong and clear'

Buddha, founder of Buddhism

I am sure by now you'll be feeling more energetic,
have lost weight and be eating well, and I've no
doubt your friends and family are noticing changes
in you. There is a positive change to the way you
are talking, thinking and dealing with life.

So today let's reflect upon our health. Many of
us take our health for granted, until the day we lose
it, and then we'll try whatever we can to get it back.
Prevention is better than cure – I am sure you are
no stranger to this concept. Prevention is *always*
better than cure. We can prevent much of the ill
health that is prevalent in modern society by
watching our diet and taking regular exercise.

Nature spent 240 million years refining and
developing this body that you inhabit. It is quite the
most sophisticated, complex piece of machinery in
the universe. It is tough, resilient and long-lasting;
it is self-regenerating and to an extent self-healing.
But if we abuse it long enough, it will shut down
much earlier than it was designed to.

**Research into longevity shows a very strong
correlation between diet and exercise as major
contributing factors to long life and good
health.**

As you move into the last quarter of the challenge you may be dreaming of having a long lie-in
one morning or eating some off-limits food, and
quite right too. The main consideration is to
recognise that we need balance in our lives. To put
yourself on a tough health regime for the rest of
your life would be a very daunting task indeed. It
would be hardship. So we have to balance what we

do with the quality of life we want to enjoy. For some people who are determined and whose physical health is their prime consideration it's not such a hardship.

Fitness is a habit for life

Once you successfully complete the 42 days, you will react in one of two possible ways. One is going to be 'fantastic': you will tick the box, turn to the people who supported you or didn't support you and say, 'I did it. I did the challenge.' You'll look great, you'll feel great, but once you tick the box you'll go back to the old habits that slowly but surely re-enter your life one by one over a short period. Three to four months later you'll be back to where you began. Or you'll be fantastically happy you did it, and you'll understand what it was all about. **What it's all about is getting back in control, making the choices to create the life you want and then taking action towards making those choices real.** Your physical health is so important. It is one of the cornerstones of the challenge.

> Your body is the only one you are ever going to have – look after it

There is an old saying: 'Use it or lose it.' When it comes to physical conditioning that saying reveals its truth. So, you need to develop the exercise habit; you need to find the opportunities to work out. Often if I am travelling and I get to a hotel where there is no gym, I will go for a 35- to 40-minute walk. I will come back to my room and I may do some sit-ups or some push-ups. I will try to use the stairs instead of the lifts; I will do something physical. Every year I set myself one maybe even two extreme physical challenges: long-distance endurance hiking, an expedition or marathons. I have discovered that to get physically fit the best thing you can do is set yourself a goal that gives the exercise purpose. I can go running or to the gym because I know in three or six months' time when I face the physical challenge all the exercise will help me. **To stay healthy we need to focus our health plan towards a goal, which is why I would encourage you to set yourself physical challenges throughout the year** – nothing too extreme, just a good target to aim for. It will give meaning and purpose to the exercise and it will no longer be a dull, dreary experience that you would rather avoid or end as quickly as possible.

Mental wellbeing benefits from mental stimulation

Consider too your mental health on a day-to-day basis, and I'm not talking about people who have mental illness, which is something different, and requires the intervention of medical practitioners or healers. Mental health for you is getting your brain to work to the best of its ability. Again, use it or lose it. Do crosswords, do puzzles, use daily visualisation exercises to stimulate the visual part of your brain. Don't read garbage or junk all the time because that's what you'll fill your head with. Read inspiring books, watch joyful and funny films. Go on courses and learn something new. Engage in stimulating conversations, read interesting books which inform and inspire you.

Spiritual exercise is not to be ignored

Your spiritual health is important too; practise your religious faith whatever that might be, but practise it with a daily devotion – it may be two or three minutes of meditation, it may be 15 minutes of prayer three times a day. Love unconditionally, open your heart to the experience of love in the world and you will find your soul sings. Practise daily simple acts of kindness and charity.

Your health requires you to engage in being aware of your current level of physical, mental and spiritual wellbeing. So every day be sure to do something to maintain and improve on the current levels of your physical, mental and spiritual health.

Do your best to maintain good health at all times and you will see the benefits throughout your life.

Today

Think of your health in terms of body, mind and spirit.

Gratitude

'Gratitude is happiness
doubled by wonder'

G. K. Chesterton, British writer, critic, 1874–1936

Have you ever done something for another person only for that person not to thank you but to be completely indifferent to the effort you made? How does it make you feel? Angry? Aggrieved? Disappointed? Anyway, their complete lack of gratitude can be hurtful. It suggests that you don't matter to them.

> We should never take other people for granted and we shouldn't take our own lives for granted

Negative people go through life completely asleep; they never wake up to the realities and the opportunities that exist all around them. They see life as one long struggle. They see life as a collection of experiences to find fault with. They are ungrateful for the small favours that come their way and dismiss so much help that is offered to them because they cannot see the wood for the trees.

Blame is lack of responsibility

Along the way this behaviour has kept them imprisoned and blinded them to the opportunities around them, creating a situation from which they have magically absolved themselves from taking responsibility. They will continually blame their circumstances for their lack of success. They never appreciate what they have; they only bemoan and focus on what they don't have.

Today I want us to look at the notion of gratitude. I know people who do not say thank you to a taxi driver or a waitress because they feel they have paid for the service and that person is only doing their job. They see the world only from their point of view. Often when they do say thank you it is used as language to effect a response. It is not from the heart.

> Research has shown that the number-one motivator in life for the average person is the need to feel appreciated

We focus so often on what we do not have, when our focus should be on what we do have, and on being thankful for the good things in our lives.

Too often we take ourselves for granted. When other people take us for granted, we feel used; we feel less valued. So you should make a big effort not to be a person who makes others feel used or less valued. You should make a very big effort today and every day of your life to make everyone you come into contact with have a good, positive experience and whenever the opportunity arises to show your gratitude.

Show you care

I've met people who never compliment others. I've played in golf matches where people are incapable of saying 'good shot' or 'well played'; it's not their way. They feel they are weakening themselves by paying a compliment. I was brought up to always say please and thank you, and I find them to be two of the most magical expressions in the world. Wherever I go, they are universal. I don't suggest you lie or give praise or thanks when none is deserved, but I do mean engage with others. Acknowledge people, let them know you are aware. Let them know what they say is important and make sure that the time you spend together is as good as it can be.

Words contain the power to influence us emotionally, both positively and negatively. We've all been at the receiving end of praise and it makes us feel good. We've also been at the receiving end of criticism, whether deserved or undeserved, and it doesn't make us feel good.

Demonstrate gratitude, receive gratitude; it is that simple

There are people who always appear ungrateful and miserable. They would protest to the contrary, but though they would not admit it they have chosen to be so. They could change that in a moment if they wanted to, but they don't because their behaviour has become habitual, and they are unwilling to accept responsibility for their actions. And until they do, change will be impossible.

Reasons to be cheerful

Reflect on all the things in your life you can be grateful for: your friends, your partner, your children, your job, the sunshine, your health, good neighbours, your food, your car, the joy you experience. You will discover there's a lot more in your life to be grateful for than you had ever previously realised.

The gratitude in life that you give will make a difference to the receiver as well as the giver.

Today

Demonstrate simple acts of gratitude to others.

Connect to Life

'You are not here merely to make a living. You are here to enable the world to live more amply, with greater vision, and with a finer spirit of hope and achievement. You are here to enrich the world. You impoverish yourself if you forget this errand'

Woodrow Wilson, US President, 1856–1924

Though we go through our life alone, we do not live in isolation, we live in separation. And though we live in separation we interconnect with the world. Every spiritual master from every religious tradition talks of one reality, known by many names: the most familiar is God, but also Universal Spirit, Love, Supreme Being, Divine Intelligence. There are many names for this one reality, and it is in this reality that we all connect as one. Yet so many people get bent all out of shape insisting that their truth is the only truth, their God is the only God. Witness the conflict and the wars that are fought for that supremacy and one would quickly conclude that something's not right. There is one eternal reality, one truth — there always has been, always will be. Whether we find it for ourselves or whether we agree with others does not change that reality, it lies beyond thought. It is not an intellectual exercise that once explained makes perfect logical sense, because it is not governed by physical laws. It is beyond knowing, yet it is within our experience to grasp and connect to it. Very few of us ever do, because we live on the surface, in the physical realm of the world.

Meditation allows us to deeply relax physically then slowly still our mind to a point where there is no thought. It is at this point of meditation that religious practitioners and mystics say that you can glimpse the eternal reality. When I was first exposed to this it made no sense to me at all. I didn't find it spooky, I just didn't understand it. It was something I thought you either believed in or you didn't, a bit like UFOs; some people believe in them, some people don't. The proof that's being presented convinces some, it doesn't convince others.

> It is in deep silence and stillness that we discover the true nature of our being

Be aware of the spiritual dimension in your life

I mention this at this point in the 42-Day Challenge because I know there is a spiritual dimension to who we are, and that we are all connected through this dimension, though very few of us ever truly get a glimpse of it. You are part of the universe and when you die the atoms that make up your body, and have made up your body throughout your lifetime, don't disappear, they change form and end up somewhere else. They might be in another body, they might be floating in the sky, so we know quite clearly from the scientific research that we are not our bodies.

If you lose a leg you don't stop being the person you were. Your mind, the ego that exists within you or exists within the brain, ceases to function when we die. So therefore we can assume that we are not our minds. So 'we' are not our minds and we are not our bodies. **Yet your spirit, that invisible force, that energy that exists and always has existed and is within us during our physical life, that spirit that your parents saw the moment you opened your eyes for the very first time and communicated itself in profound deep love, that spirit never dies.**

Because we cannot see the spirit, it is very easy to dismiss it as just another UFO-type experience

Yet we connect with the spirit every day. We connect in acts of kindness, moments of pure joy and most often through people we meet. Those moments when we have inexplicable feelings that a person we have met is good, is kind, has some quality about them that we sense but cannot accurately explain. They are deeply spiritual, they are connected to the world in a knowing way.

I've met two people who are spiritual masters. They were not necessarily religious people by nature, but they were just totally and utterly connected. There was a wonderful warmth, compassion, humility and knowing about them. Absolute peace, no need to be boastful, not pursuing wealth, they were absolutely in tune with the world around them.

My father died when he was 52 years of age, and I was very close to him. The day he died, his body was taken away and prepared and put in a casket; the next day his body was brought back into the house and was put in the front room, as was the tradition so that people could come and pay their final respects.

I finally arrived home many hours after he had died. I didn't want to go and look at my father, because I knew it would be very upsetting. Yet when I went into the room to see him lying in his best suit I was immediately struck by the feeling that he wasn't there. My father wasn't there — he was gone. Of course the life had gone from his body, but more pertinently he wasn't there. Yet curiously on two occasions since he passed away I've had a profound sense of his presence in my life. I don't believe in ghosts, but I do believe in the eternal nature of the soul.

People talk about soul mates; they meet a person and instantly feel a strong connection to this person that they have never known before, a connection that lies at the level of the soul. It is not about beauty, status and money; it is about a deeper understanding that we cannot adequately explain. **So reflect upon what you believe the nature of your soul may be, even if up until now you don't believe you have one at all.**

Truth exists irrespective of what we may believe

I've written before that if you believe in God, or whether you believe you have a soul or not, it does not change the truth. If you believe then you will see the connections with your life more clearly, with people you meet, experiences you have, coincidences that occur. You will put them into the context of your learning about yourself and your overall life experience. If you don't believe, that's fine. You probably won't see them; you're not looking for them. But I would ask you to be open to them. Keep an open mind, practise meditation and ask the universe for what you want, and then, based on the experiences that follow, decide for yourself if things have changed or not.

If we do physical exercise, we know that we become healthy and strong. We know that if we eat well, the right food, we will improve our wellbeing and maintain the right weight, and our bodies will function well. Is it therefore so great a leap of the imagination to accept that if you do spiritual exercises regularly, you too will discover a deeper truth? That's when the magic really begins.

I cannot even begin to explain this to any degree of satisfaction, any more than I could exactly describe a colour to a person blind from birth. Because words are wholly inadequate, because it is a mystery, and not one that reveals itself to scientific investigation, because it exists beyond physical laws, for many people that single concept is the stumbling block. So it has to be an act of faith. Suffice it to say, that if you earnestly and honestly seek out this reality, this universal truth, you will discover it.

You are not separate from the
universe or the world around you,
you are a part of it.

Today

Be aware of your oneness with
the world around you.

Tough it Out

'He who can't endure the bad will not live to see the good'

Yiddish proverb

When she was 80 years old, my mother went into hospital for major heart surgery. She was naturally anxious about the operation that lay ahead of her. Whenever I visited her, I tried to speak to her words of comfort and support, and before I left would always remind her she was not to worry because I knew was she was tough. We would laugh about it, but I was always trying to place in her mind the notion that she indeed was tough. I visited her the night before her operation and told her that I would see her the next day.

The operation went as well as could possibly have been hoped for – a resounding success, and she was returned to her bed in the ward. I went to see her, and she looked somewhat bedraggled, having had major heart surgery. She was sitting in bed and I said, 'Well done, you look great.' She looked at me and she said, 'Robin, I'm all toughed out.' And then she laughed. It became her catch-phrase for the next couple of months; whenever she felt tired she would look at me and laugh as she said, 'I'm all toughed out.' It became a standing joke that stopped her feeling sorry for herself at a time when the experience had felt too much.

The reality is we don't run out of compassion, we don't run out of kindness, we don't run out of love and we don't run out of toughness – the deep-down mental toughness that you have demonstrated throughout this challenge.

We all have different thresholds of pain. One person's discomfort is another person's agony. But your success will require that at times you be tough on yourself. There will be moments when you want to give it up because the pain sometimes can just become a little too much. Sometimes the diet can just be a little too severe, and that is when our character is tested. And that is the time that we want to look into ourselves and remind ourselves that we are tough enough and can really do this.

> Your ability to tough it out is greater than you imagine, and reveals itself when you simply don't just give up at the first hurdle

No doubt on the journey so far you will have been tempted. When we give in to temptation, it feels good for a brief moment – then the regret follows. The easiest thing in the world is to justify our actions, excuse our behaviour and give in to temptation.

If you don't give in to temptation your mental toughness will be increased just a little bit each time, which in turn is reflected in a more positive self-image, that grows and grows.

Staying power

A friend of mine, whom I've known for over 30 years, told me that as a schoolboy he decided that he would stay fit for his entire life. He set himself a goal of doing 50 sit-ups and 50 push-ups every day for the rest of his life. He is now 50 years of age and he still has the physique he had when he was in his twenties. Has he missed his exercises in the past 30 years? Yes, on a number of occasions, but very rarely. I asked him if he found it easy to do his daily exercise regime and he replied, 'No, it's tough.' He said when he's tired or running late the last thing he wants to do is to get down and do 50 push-ups and 50 sit-ups, but having done it every day he feels good about himself and proud of sticking to his promise made thirty years earlier.

When those lazy moments catch you off guard don't give in to them

Be immensely proud of how far you have come. Your success so far has not just happened by chance. You made this happen. You have taken responsibility to become the architect of your own success. You really do have the resilience and mental toughness to deal with every obstacle you encounter and to overcome it.

Do the right thing

I've never ever regretted doing the right thing, sticking to my plan, even in the face of repeated failure. My regrets have always been over giving up too early, making excuses and letting myself and others down. I now realise the secret was just to do it, and not to worry about being toughed out, because that can never happen, as my mother proved and life continues to prove to me.

Toughness is a state of mind, and
you are mentally much tougher
than you imagine.

Today

Whatever challenges you face today –
know that you can overcome them.

Don't Worry

'What a pity that so many people would rather believe their doubts and doubt their beliefs . . . Why don't we just decide to have no doubts, and believe our beliefs! Fear and worry is just the misuse of the creative powers'

Anon

M y most overused expression is 'don't worry'. I am forever telling myself and others not to worry. Worrying doesn't fix things and it doesn't get things done. It doesn't make things better and it certainly does not affect the outcome. It is a natural state of mild anxiety. It is a recurring thought that can just sit in our head and spin round and round and round. It pulls us down, it saps our energy, it makes us fearful for the future. Worry and fear are closely related. If we worry enough the worry can turn into fear, which is bad for our health: it affects our ability to enjoy ourselves, to sleep well, it increases our dependency on the use of external substances – tea, coffee, alcohol, cigarettes and worse. We make ourselves ill; we age faster. A state of worry is not a good state to be in.

As you have gone through the 42-Day Challenge, I am sure you have had moments of doubt and even fear. Could you stay the course? Let's put fear and worry in context.

99% of the things we fear never happen

What is it you fear? We all may imagine we have different fears and anxieties, but deep down inside I suspect our fears are very similar. **We are afraid of being unloved, of being alone, of being unhappy, of serious illness, of poverty, of mental illness, of being the victim of crime; we're afraid** of rejection, losing our jobs, being made un-welcome in our social group, and, everybody's favourite, dying. I am sure you can add to that. The irony is that 99% of the things we fear never happen. And here's an even stranger strange irony. **When the thing you fear happens, you will deal with it.**

> When the thing you fear happens, you will discover inner strength and you will deal with it

When something you fear happens, I promise you will not lie down and curl up in a ball and give up on life. You will stand up and face it to the best of your ability. You will heal and you will grow. Many people when they face their fears overcome them and end up wondering what they had been afraid of in the first place.

Deconstructing your fears

How do you overcome your fears? Whatever it is you fear the first thing you need to do is decon-struct it. You created it in your mind. You've given it thought, and by giving it thought you have built it up into a bigger and bigger reality, which you seek to avoid. You probably did this unwittingly, so what you need to do now is deconstruct it. First we need to examine where our fears come from.

As a child you may have been told that if you didn't get a good job you would end up homeless and lonely. You may have been told that you were unlovable, that no one would want to marry you. These negative thoughts about ourselves and our future were embedded in our minds many years ago and surface at times of stress. After a while they stay on the surface and we end up thinking about them all the time.

> Don't dwell on the things over which you have no control

Maybe you were told that you would be unlovable and as a result whenever you get into a relationship this deeply embedded thought makes you suspicious of the other person's intentions, or you simply expect to be abandoned. Because of this, you act in accordance with those beliefs, and guess what happens yet again: the relationship breaks down.

Deconstruct your fears and replace them with understanding

We can deconstruct negative thoughts and beliefs, reprogramme them and replace them. My advice is to face fears head on, and, better still, experience what it is that you fear, let it happen. You will discover that it really was not so bad.

You will discover that it doesn't really exist other than in your mind. I'm not suggesting that if you fear being run over by a bus, you should go and get run over by a bus – that would be stupid. I do believe that if you fear poverty, abandonment, loneliness, cancer, or whatever it is, you should learn a little bit more about it, look at the probabilities of it happening, speak to people to whom it has happened, read their life stories. For everything you fear, there is someone who has gone through it and come out the other side; as you learn more and more about it, your confidence grows.

I used to joke that I didn't have a fear of heights, I just had a fear of hitting the ground. So I used to look for opportunities where I could deconstruct that fear. I would talk to people who worked on the outside of high buildings, I spoke to mountaineers and rock climbers. I even started to do a little rock climbing myself and I realised that my fear, though natural, was irrational. Since then I can honestly say that I've put this fear into perspective and rationalised my understanding.

Identify your irrational fears

As you move towards completing your 42 days, I would like you to reflect on what you currently are afraid of in your life and in the future. You will discover that there are rational fears concerning death and suffering. There are things that we will naturally fear, which are outside our control. But don't dwell on the things over which you have no control. **Instead examine those other fears you hold and you may discover that a lot of them are irrational – such as not being good enough, that you are unlovable, that people will reject you, that you'll end up homeless. You have no evidence of any kind to suggest that these things are going to happen.**

Don't worry – be happy. If you can be happy, it is difficult to worry. Worrying and happiness do not co-exist.

Remember

Worrying doesn't fix things; when you find yourself worrying tell yourself that it will pass.

Today

Examine your fears and if there is no evidence to support them, deconstruct them.

Power

'Most powerful is he who has himself in his own power'

Seneca, Roman philosopher and politician, 5 BC–65

As we move towards completing the 42 days I have no doubt you will have undergone many different emotions, and know you will be thinking of the future and carrying forward the lessons from the challenge.

Self-determination

You have exercised self-determination every hour of the challenge; you have made conscious choices to follow the conditions of the challenge and your personal plans to realise your goals. At every moment you had an option to continue or to give up, to see it through or to make an excuse. You were in control of your decisions, which is where your true power lies. We often mistake power simply for physical or mental strength, whereas our personal power is found in our ability to control our thoughts and actions and take responsibility for our lives. **The more responsibility and self-control we demonstrate the more personal power we experience.**

Be an independent thinker and doer

There are people who have what is referred to as 'learned dependence'; in short, they have for so long had others take care of or provide for them that they don't know how to do it for themselves. It often happens in the early teenage years where children have a parent who still does everything for them, and as a result they don't learn how to do it for themselves. A simple example could be cooking. I have met many people who can't cook — they never learned and when asked will tell you that they can't. As a result of this they will be dependent on others to cook or prepare their food, be it in a fast-food joint, a restaurant or in the form of a ready-made meal in a supermarket, they depend on others to provide. Obviously cooking is a simple example, but if you extrapolate the principles behind learned dependency, you can suddenly understand why for some people the simple aspects of life that we take for granted appear as impossible challenges.

> Power is not simply a measure of strength, it is a reflection of our self-control and self-determination

Just as no child has ever learned to run before it learned to crawl, as it is simply impossible, **so too in our lives we have to move from dependent, where we have little power, to independent, where our true power lies**. It is important that we become independent thinkers, and don't simply follow the popular view or the opinions of others simply to 'fit in'.

As a consequence of thinking for ourselves we

have a second choice to make, which is, 'Do I turn my thoughts into action?'. It may appear that the answer is an obvious yes, but you would be surprised by how many people simply do nothing about it. They figure things have worked out just fine without taking action, so why bother. Take the person who says they can't cook. They could learn, they could go to night classes, or attend a cookery school, they could buy instructional videos or any one of a hundred simplified cookery books, but they tell you it's just not that important to them. But when you probe further they tell you that they just can't, and the reason they can't is because they believe their conditioning.

Your life, your choice

We have choices to make every day and generally need to keep our eyes fixed on the goal we seek, because, I'm sorry to say, and it's a fact of life, most people take the easy option and give up. The easy option is giving in to temptation and giving up on hardship. So if you have a choice between getting up at 6 a.m. and starting the day with a series of tasks, to create control in your life and achieve lifelong ambitions, and staying in bed, the majority of people would roll over and stay in bed. They are giving in to the temptation of extra sleep, because they are not thinking or acting on the goal they have set. So too in your life every choice you make is ultimately going to move you closer to realising your goal (getting up at 6 a.m. if that is part of your plan) or move you further away from your goal or slow down your progress (staying in bed and going back to sleep). It is your choice. It's easy to blame others or our circumstances to excuse our inaction, but we know that in reality we are only fooling ourselves. **One day it finally dawns on us, we have procrastinated all the way to old age, and though it is never too late to change, sometimes it is too late to take action.**

Personal power gets things done

The more you determine to take action on your thoughts and follow your plan to the letter, the more you will achieve and the faster you will progress. As this transformation occurs your confidence grows, as your confidence grows so too your power grows, and in turn your confidence grows again, and a positive transformational upward spiral develops. By contrast when you do not follow through, give up or make endless excuses, your confidence takes a knock and your power diminishes. You stop believing in yourself, you become more dependent on others to make you feel good, to achieve your goals, to make you feel loved, capable and worthy; eventually you end up feeling powerless and a victim. I don't mean this to sound gloomy and I know that you will be in the upward spiral, but **I want you to** be aware that you are either in the process of moving forward by exercising the power of independent thought and action, or you are going backwards.

Turn positive thoughts into positive actions and your confidence and personal sense of power will flourish

Treat yourself as you would your best friend

Do you like yourself? It may seem like a strange question this far into the challenge, but it is worth examining how you feel about yourself. The way you feel about yourself will have a huge impact on the level to which you are able to achieve. If you have a good self-image you will think, feel and speak positively about yourself; if you have a poor self-image you will think and feel negatively about yourself. This in turn impacts on how you respond to the choices you make. If you have a positive self-image, you will feel that you are capable and worthy of the success you seek, and you will take action, as you believe you deserve to succeed and can see the point of the actions you take. If you have a negative self-image, you will feel unworthy; you'll tell yourself that you will probably fail so what is the point in trying anyway: your failure habit kicks in again.

> Treat and think of yourself as you think of your best friend, someone you like whose company you enjoy

So, simple as it sounds, *like* yourself. If you **identify traits or aspects within yourself that you know would irritate you if manifest in another person, consciously determine first through thought, then through action to change them**. It really is that simple, it's not easy unlearning the habits of a lifetime but it is simple, and achievable.

The personal power that enables you to become independent and complete as a person is not given to you, you already possess it, you just didn't realise it. The control this power gives you is over yourself and how you experience this life journey. So don't give in now or in the future to the opportunity every moment offers you: live life to the full and **have no regrets.**

Power is not simply about physical, mental or financial strength, it is about being in control of your life and taking responsibility for the choices you make.

Today

Ask yourself whether your choices are moving you closer to or further away from your goals.

Reach Out

'For it is in giving that we receive'

Saint Francis of Assisi, 1182–1226

As you come to the last few days and hours of the 42 days, I want you to look far beyond the end of the challenge. Look to the future and set ambitious goals for your life targets for yourself. Aim higher than you previously had dared to. Dream bigger dreams than you had imagined possible. Look at the canvas of life that lies in front of you and determine all the marvellous things you wish to paint on it, and in so doing positively touch the lives of others by your actions.

> Everything you do in life will have consequences good or bad and that will be a result of the intention that you put into the actions

I am sure you have now changed the way you see yourself, and more importantly you think differently about your potential in terms of what you can achieve with your life. So I ask you now to reach out. Reach out to others, and equally ask for help when you need it. I regularly ask for advice, information and help whenever I need it, and if the person I ask cannot help me, more often than not they will guide me towards someone who can.

Always be a student of life

Think of yourself as a student, always curious, questioning, learning. Never stop learning. When someone asks for your help, don't hesitate to give it. To the best of my ability I answer every email I receive, and when people call me up for advice, if it is possible to spend time with them I will do so, or I will arrange to talk with them on the phone.

You can have a profound impact on the lives of other people by the simplest of your actions. Your actions don't need to be dramatic, they don't need to be front page news, but they need to be made with the intention of helping and making a difference in the lives of others in the world around you.

Too often we find ourselves looking inward, thinking about what's wrong and what we cannot do. This is OK as it makes us aware of the facts and the realistic limitations of our lives and it can put things into perspective. But once done, give your head a rest and focus your attention on the things you can do. There's an old quotation that says, 'Go out on a limb, that's where the fruit is.' Too often we stay in our comfort zone because it's safe, it's secure. I know that even though you've all gone beyond the limits of your previous comfort zone there is a danger that, becoming complacent and feeling you have done enough, you'll return to it.

Always be on the lookout for opportunity

I want you to be an explorer, I want you to seek out those things that you really want to do, no matter how extreme or silly they may appear to other people. The fact that you want to do them is all that is important, but you need to reach out beyond your comfort zone. Stretch the boundary of your imagination as often as you can and determine to give 100% of your effort to making it happen.

> When you reach out to life and take that first step, the universe will become your partner and teach you the rest of the dance

Over the past five weeks you have changed how you feel about yourself and what you believe you are capable of. There is no limit to what you can do now. This is a new world of opportunities that you are opening up. It is very easy to be cynical, to dismiss a lot of the sentiments and the intentions of the past six weeks as just feelgood words that don't really apply to you, but if you've applied yourself with diligence, trust, faith, confidence and a positive attitude, you will see and know the difference. But to change your life and explore the opportunities and create your success you need to take a leap of faith. You have got to have true faith in yourself. Faith is the ability to believe in something for which there is no evidence. You have to take the leap of faith in the knowledge that you will be fine: that everything will be all right, that should your fears appear you will overcome them, that should something go wrong you will cope.

A Japanese encounter

In 2004 I went for two weeks to explore Japan. It's a country I'd always wanted to visit and I travelled on my own with a little backpack. I went to Nagasaki to visit the site of the second atomic bomb that was dropped in the Second World War. I wandered around the town for two days and visited certain shrines, and I sat in cafés. I went for a walk down by the docks. It's not an especially pretty town – there are things to see, but it has an industrial heritage. I ate in simple noodle bars because they had pictorial menus I could point to as I cannot read Japanese, and on the second night, as I was walking back to my Japanese hotel, which had a curfew of 11 o'clock in the evening, I saw a little restaurant. I didn't know if it was fish or meat or pork noodles or dumplings because I didn't know what was inside. I pulled the curtain back and as I walked in I saw a very small restaurant. The waitress, who was in her mid-50s, smiled and welcomed me but was a little surprised to see me. The chef behind the counter gave me a wonderful smile, and beckoned me forth. They handed me a menu entirely in Japanese and there were no pictures to be seen. It was a moment when one could feel uncomfortable. I certainly did, so I asked for a beer, as I knew how to say that. They started to ask me some questions as to what I would like. I pointed to other people's plates and the chef began. There was a woman sitting next to me who gave me a pair of chopsticks and picked up a piece of food from her dish which she gave to me to try. It was mackerel; it was delicious. I spent the next two hours doing my best to communicate with these people by smiling, being silly, enjoying the food and their company. We got out a map of the world and I showed them where I came from and we had a wonderful time. I had a little phrase book, which was very limited, but I indicated to them that I had had a nice meal and would be back the next night.

The next day I had spent the day wandering around Nagasaki. Walking back to the hotel, I realised I was not so hungry, but felt I should drop by and say hello, yet I felt very self-conscious. Once more I was going into a situation where I could not speak any Japanese, to a little restaurant where I would not know what to order. I didn't really want to get out of my comfort zone but I did. The reason I did was because I had said I would see them. I knew that I would honour what I had said, but only for 20 minutes, and then I would leave. When I went in, they were delighted to see me, as though I was an old-time friend. As I sat down not only did they put a beer beside me, they opened a special bottle of chilled sake and gave me a glass.

There was a man sitting next to me at the counter. He turned to me and in perfect English said, 'Where are you from?' He then interpreted for the next hour to his friends everything I said. I was reaching out without a sense of awkwardness and self-consciousness; I was in the moment, sharing life; photographs were taken, cards were signed and a great time was had. I told them that I would come back, and one day I will. Our lives interconnected and have changed a little bit from meeting each other, and we all have a memory and a powerful experience of friendship; we crossed the language and cultural divide.

Learning new steps

You have to join in the dance of life to experience the steps. Once you join in the dance you learn the steps. When you reach out to life and take that first step, the universe will become your partner and teach you the rest of the dance.

Though I know you are familiar with the consequences of taking action I want you to think today about the need to reach out beyond your comfort zone. Lift yourself up beyond the average, don't settle for mediocrity, life is an adventure, and it doesn't matter what age we are, what our situation or our circumstances, there is always something we can do to change the situation, even if it is only to change our attitude.

How many friends do you know still waiting for something wonderful to happen in their life, who are forever putting off until tomorrow the plans and dreams they held as young people, then as middle-aged people, and eventually as old people? Even for them, it's still not too late. They still believe that as long as they're talking, they are keeping the dream alive and one day, some day, their dream will just happen. Until one day they discover it's too late, that it doesn't just happen, you have to make it happen. So don't waste time. Don't sell yourself short. We have to be bold and have faith if we are going to reach for our stars. Remember **if you believe you can, you can**.

It is through stretching ourselves
that we grow.

Today

If you are asked for help or assistance,
give it freely and with compassion.

Courage

'Courage and perseverance have a magic talisman, before which obstacles vanish into thin air'

John Quincy Adams, US President, 1767–1848

Today I would like you to reflect upon the notion of courage, and specifically your courage. You have come a long way since you began the challenge, when I am sure you experienced uncertainty as to whether you would succeed or fail. Whenever we face a challenge in our lives, be it big or small, we need to have courage and risk failure in the pursuit of our success.

You fall – you get up, no big deal

The quotation at the start of this reflection talks about courage and perseverance, which is what we require to change our lives. **The courage to risk failure and the ability to try again and again and again, to never give up on ourselves, stands like a signpost on the road to success and personal transformation.** You have begun a journey I sincerely hope will continue for the rest of your life; and you believe you are indeed courageous, because you have dared to fail, and got up every time you fell.

I want you to think of courage as a quality that you possess and have actively engaged over the past 38 days, it is not a quality we would commonly use to describe ourselves, but it is a quality you have demonstrated many times over the past five and a half weeks. Because for the past 38 days you have pushed yourself out of your comfort zone.

It is not about heroics

For me courage is not simply about uncommon bravery, which we admire. Courage is acknowledging that there is a risk that you might fail but trying anyway. In the final analysis **if we never try we will never know**. Now, some people are content never to know; they have all the reasons in the world why they never chased their dreams, because failure is for them too painful, and the consequences too damaging. So they don't try. I don't know about you, but many times in my past I have hesitated, made excuses, continued to plan endlessly, waited for the time to be right and, as always intended, taken no action. I just kept talking about what I was going to do. I could always justify my inaction, I could always absolve myself of responsibility. In truth I was just plain scared of failing.

> Personal courage to move out of your comfort zone will give rise to increased confidence, and expose you to many previously unseen opportunities

It was after I had cancer that I came to realise that nothing changes until we take action. I had experienced much failure in my life, and one way or another it always hurt: a broken heart, a failed exam, rejection, losing in sport, being excluded, and a host of other experiences. So I took the easy way out. I stopped trying, and when I stopped trying, guess what? Nothing happened. You see if you don't try you absolutely cannot fail, but you most certainly cannot succeed either. **To win the game of life, love, health or wealth you have to be in the game.** Yet so many people sit passively as observers, forever justifying their lack of action with one of the hundred and one excuses they have used all their lives.

Your courage is not determined by the outcome it is determined by the intention behind the action

Acts of kindness

One of the reasons I made performing an act of unconditional kindness each day part of the challenge, other than it being a good action in itself, was to force you on occasion to reach out to another person and risk their rejection. You may or may not have had that experience; either way, every time you sought to help another you risked them being offended, ungrateful or even hostile. The very act of reaching out exposed us to those possible outcomes; it forced you out of a natural comfort zone. So even though in the past you may not have thought you were particularly courageous in the arena of life, by reaching out to assist another person you did do something you previously may not have been comfortable or confident in doing.

Today think about other areas of your life where you are willing to push yourself through a self-imposed barrier. Think about those things that you believe you cannot achieve: a promotion at work, relocating your life to a new country, falling in love, losing weight, running a marathon, setting up your own business, singing in a choir, learning a language, in fact whatever you have ever wished for, but for reasons unknown have convinced yourself that you cannot succeed at — because you have convinced yourself that failure is inevitable, or perhaps you are just plain scared. I want you to identify one thing that you still believe you cannot do, and remind yourself that you in fact possess courage; and trust in that courage to get you through those irrational fears.

> Failure is only painful when we give up trying

Never give up

A common theme of those who realise their dreams and achieve seemingly impossible goals is that they never gave up. Yet how many people did just that when they were only moments away from success, but never realised it. They stopped believing that they could make it, they gave up because the struggles became too hard. There are moments when life becomes hard, and our determination and resolve, battered and bruised by constant failure, setback and disappointment, simply have had enough, when giving up is not only easy, it becomes a release from confidence-sapping hardship and despair. I am sure you have experienced or witnessed it yourself. So with the best will in the world someone telling you to keep your chin up, stay positive, be brave and keep going isn't really going to do it, no matter how well intentioned the encouragement. Rather I believe we need to take time to rest, just long enough to gather our thoughts and rest our bodies, and remind ourselves of the purpose that lies behind the realisation of our goal. We need to keep the dream alive, we need to remember why we started in the first place, and we need if necessary to change our plan. **We need to believe that we will succeed, and that is where your courage will support you through those difficult times, and failure will be put in context, and you will once more try again and not give up.**

We may not be able to win every time, but we can do our best, and live with the knowledge we tried

Onwards and upwards

For the past 38 days you have taken hundreds of conscious actions, some easy, others hard. People variously have supported you or waited for you to fail, but you are still on the challenge, you are still standing, taller and more in control than ever before. Your success has not been a matter of luck, it has been due to you having the courage and perseverance to create your own magic.

Courage is also about moving out
of your comfort zone and being
willing to fail.

Today

Think of courage as one of your
personal qualities and experience
it in your actions.

Live in the Now

'When I look back now over my life and call to mind what I might have had simply for taking and did not take, my heart is like to break'

Akhenaton, Egyptian king, died c. 1354 BC

We have no problem at all understanding that the past is gone, we cannot return to it. We can remember it if we choose to, but it is gone. The future is, as they say, but a dream; it does not exist either, other than in our imagination.

> Life is a here and now experience and everything else is either a memory or a promise

We should seek our happiness in the present moment, not make it conditional on future events, and neither should we cause ourselves to be unhappy by constantly reliving painful experiences that happened in our past and unwittingly using them as a template for the future.

> You get the most out of life by being fully present to what is going on around you, in thought, feeling and action

Seek to be fully alive

Psychologists say that people who participate in high-risk sports like motor racing or rock climbing experience those intense moments where everything around them disappears and their attention is in the present moment. Sometimes this is referred to as being 'in the zone', when all sense of time and place disappears. People who participate in high-risk sports do not have a death wish. What they do have is the need to be fully alive, and it is in those moments of heightened awareness that life shows itself in its fullness. I think it is difficult in our everyday lives to reach those extraordinary levels where time stands still and our appreciation of the experience is one with the moment.

However, you can direct your attention to where you are and concentrate fully on what you are doing, be fully attentive to whoever you are with and appreciate the moments and experiences that every moment creates.

> It is our thoughts in combination with our actions that determine our future

Therefore, when you are speaking to somebody give them 100% of your attention. Listen to them attentively, understand what they are saying, empathise with their situation.

When you meditate, take the time to appreciate the full impact of what you are trying to do in your meditation. Concentrate on the stillness and deep relaxation you seek to achieve, don't spend half the meditation thinking about dinner 20 minutes off. Be fully engaged. We only have this moment in our lives. It is here that life is, the future, for all its uncertainty, does not exist.

People look for magical shortcuts to success and happiness and in so doing miss the obvious clues that will assist them. What gives us the greatest assistance is our connection to the present moment.

Success is not a destination; it is an experience of the journey. And it is up to us to make sure that every moment of the journey is lived fully in the experiences of the present moment.

Our life is divided into three terms: that which was, that which is and that which will be. Let us learn from the past and profit by the present and from the present, to live a better future.

The past is gone, the future does not exist, all we ever have is the present moment, so always be fully present in that moment.

Today

Raise your awareness throughout the day to being fully present in the now.

Finding Peace

'A crust eaten in peace is better than a banquet partaken in anxiety'

Aesop, Greek writer, 620 BC–560 BC

What do you think of when you think of peace? Its most common usage tends to suggest a state where there is no war, or absence of noise or a feeling of personal relaxation.

I believe peace is a state of no conflict, a state where we are balanced and have a strong sense of our oneness and do not resist life, either mentally, emotionally or spiritually. Have you ever had a moment in your life that you wished would last for ever? Moments of joy, laughter and love?

By now as you have moved through the challenge, you understand that you have 100% control over how you react to life. You also know that when you take action, you create change. **It is for us to choose to be at peace with the world, and not be frustrated by the actions of others or allow ourselves to continually get angry.** It is not for us to seek arguments with others because they have upset us. It is more important we remain at peace with ourselves and with life even though people may do things that cause us upset and even distress. It is when we can remain balanced and at peace that we are most able to make the right choice and have the best response.

You can choose to be at peace

The irony is that to create change in our lives we have to take action, yet to achieve inner peace we need to do nothing at all, we need simply to be. We need to stop resisting and start being present to the experience.

Peace is found 'in' us. When you meditate deeply you feel a wonderful calm and indeed a sense of peace, which is emotional and spiritual. You sense that wonderful calm and peace that exist at the core of your being. We should seek to carry this feeling with us throughout the day. Things will happen and if we allow our emotions to control how we respond then we will respond emotionally and in the process lose control. If we allow our spirit to be the guiding influence then it is almost certain that our response will be peaceful, compassionate, loving and kind, because that is our spiritual nature. It enables us to see events in the context of our lives. It allows us to realise that the simple incidents that cause great frustration on a physical level are of no consequence in reality. So we must choose always, where we can, to be at peace.

I have no doubt you will take away many things from this 42 days and I hope that you will keep them for the rest of your lives. So be at peace, and carry it with you throughout your life. Share your peace with others; you will influence their lives, you will be that oasis of calm in a world of turmoil. Speak with peace; speak with compassion and understanding. **All the skills you need to be happy are within you.**

Through your example others will be inspired and be influenced. What you give in life, as we have discussed many times, you get back with interest. So today as we move towards the final day of the challenge, I want you to reflect on this: **give peace by being peaceful wherever you can, to whoever you can, whenever you can.**

Peace is absence of conflict.

Today

Let nothing bother you, remain in a
state of peace and calm from your
meditation and carry it through
the day.

You Can Do Anything

'If I were to wish for anything, I should not wish for wealth and power, but for the passionate sense of the potential, for the eye which, ever young and ardent, sees the possible. Pleasure disappoints, possibility never. And what wine is so sparkling, what so fragrant, what so intoxicating, as possibility!'

Søren Aabye Kierkegaard, Danish religious philosopher, 1813–55

Today is the last day of the challenge. In a few hours you will have completed the 42 days that you embarked upon six weeks ago. I can think of no finer thought than to simply ask you to believe with all your heart that you can do anything. You have proved to yourself that you can take control of your life, set goals and take action. You've understood the power of visualisation and meditation, you've understood that what you eat and how you exercise will impact on your body, you've connected to your oneness with the world, the universe, and I hope discovered a sense of your own spirit.

I sincerely hope that you see today not as the end, but rather the begining of a world of infinite possibilities, no matter what you may have believed previously, and that dreams do come true. I can think of no better way to conclude the challenge than to tell you that I am delighted for you. Now you have woken up to your potential your life will never be the same again.

I'm very happy for you, and I wish you every continued success and joy for the rest of your life.

You can do anything.

Today

Really is the first day of the rest of your life. A life of endless possibilities.

Part 3

Meditation and Visualisation

One of the key principles behind the 42 days is simplicity, with meditation and visualisation being the key to the successful completion of the challenge. As long as you make time to do it, then you will reap the benefits from it immediately.

I want to describe the simple form that you will follow for 20 minutes every day, and it is the simplest form of meditation and visualisation I know. At the end of 42 days I know you will enjoy the benefits that come from meditation. At that point if you wish to go on to more advanced forms of meditation then you will be capable of doing so.

20-minute meditation routine

Every day during the first hour in the morning you will meditate and visualise for 20 minutes. You can if you wish meditate twice a day.

The simplest form of meditation that I know

- Find a space where you can be alone and in silence. Sit in a chair, upright, not slouched, feet on the floor, hands may be gently joined on your lap or resting one on either leg.
- At first you will be distracted by random thoughts, noises and external stimuli; you will also not be aware how long 20 minutes actually is, so have a clock handy.
- Close your eyes and breathe in, as you breathe in be aware of the breath coming in, then breathe out.
- Still your mind, concentrate on breathing in and breathing out. Empty your mind. Think of nothing at all. No thought, just the breath in and the breath out. No thought at all is to enter your mind. When a thought comes into your mind, do not hold on to it, concentrate on breathing in and breathing out.
- As you breathe in and out, if you wish you can add the following aspect to your meditation, which you will find very beneficial, and I would strongly recommend that you do.

  As you breathe in say quietly in your mind a positive thought, and as you slowly breathe out say quietly in your mind the opposite negative thought.

I am breathing in courage . . . I am breathing out fear
Breathing in peace . . . breathing out anxiety
Breathing in joy . . . breathing out sadness
Breathing in health . . . breathing our sickness
Breathing in wealth . . . breathing out poverty
Breathing in confidence . . . breathing out self doubt

After you have reached a feeling of physical relaxation, you begin the mental countdown to stillness.

- In your mind count back slowly from 10 to 1 each time telling yourself you are getting more and more relaxed.

10, 9, more and more relaxed
8, 7, deeper and deeper
6, 5, I am getting more and more relaxed
4, 3, deeper and deeper
2, 1, I am fully relaxed

Though you may feel self-conscious, or not fully relaxed, and continue to feel as though you cannot still your mind, with practise both the breathing exercise and the 10 to 1 countdown will act as active triggers in inducing the meditative state.

- That's it. You're meditating.

That is the basic technique of meditation. It really is this simple, and takes 3–5 minutes.

Visualising your future goals

- While you are in the state of meditation, you are ready to begin your visualisation.
- While in a state of active calm and deep relaxation, I want you to imagine your future. In your mind's eye see the goals, both long term and short term, that you have dreamed of achieving. See yourself actually experiencing them in the future, not just observing them. In your mind's eye step into the future scene you are observing, and experience the feelings and emotions you will associate with its realisation.
- While experiencing the future you seek to achieve, incorporate phrases that you can associate with this manifestation, such as, 'I am moving towards my goal', 'I will complete the task I have set myself.' Use positive, optimistic language, which is always affirmative in tone and content.

315

- Give instruction to your subconscious mind in the form of imagined future 'scenes' and positive affirmations.
- Every time you visualise revisit this imagined scene in your mind's eye. See it as clearly as you can. See it existing in the future and then, quite simply, when you are ready stop visualising and return to the state of meditation where you have no conscious thought and are simply deeply relaxed.

When you have finished the visualisation, return to the meditative state until you are ready to return to full awareness in the room.

You do this by counting forward from 1 to 10, telling yourself as you do, you are getting more and more aware.

1, 2   I am becoming more aware of my surroundings
3, 4   more alert and present
5, 6   I am coming to full awareness
7, 8   more and more aware
9, 10 I am fully present

The exact words you use are not so important, but it is best to return from the meditative state in a slow and easy manner.

In the first number of meditations you will find it almost impossible to sit still and not be distracted. Your brain has spent all of its lifetime thinking, being busy, and it doesn't like being quiet. **It is essential that you quieten it down, for it is in the silence of meditation that we can hear our heart's desire.** We can programme into our subconscious mind the future we wish to achieve and we connect with the universal consciousness that is all around us.

It is in the periods after deep meditation that I find I have the most energy and some of my best insights. **From your meditation and the visualisation, you will be focusing clearly on the goals you seek to achieve and therefore every action you take during your waking conscious hours will find its sense and its origin in the meditation and visualisation.**

Additionally, they will enable you to take the action and form the habits that you need to create the success you desire.

As you become more accomplished you can if you wish move on to more advanced techniques, but they all find their origins in the method I have just explained. Meditating and practising visualisation is just like exercise: the more you do it, the better you become.

In earlier books I have described more detailed forms of meditation and visualisation and I have brought out a series of guided visualisations on CD to help people accelerate the process. If you need more information go to my website, www.siegerinternational.com, where there are many resources that can help you. Meditation and visualisation are very simple.

42-Day Eating Plan

Rule number seven of the 42 days is no processed, convenience or junk food. The reason for this is clear. Your body has evolved over 240 million years. The digestive system evolved to use natural produce like fruit, vegetables and other natural food groups, and consequently our bodies evolved to naturally digest and absorb fully the nutrition contained therein.

Over the last 50 to 100 years, however, we have seen the introduction of preservatives, additives and a host of other elements that you may see on the labels of processed foods: 'E' numbers, colourings, antioxidants; then there are the big bad three, added salt, added sugar and high fat.

We are in fact simple creatures – our senses of smell, taste and vision have a huge influence on our desire to ingest certain foods. Animals in the wild crave fat, fat is stored in the body and used in times of hardship; this makes excellent sense. If you were a wild animal that hibernates in the winter you would require huge reserves of high-fat foods to survive.

But you're not a wild animal and you don't have to hibernate.

We do not need to store fat, yet as part of our evolutionary heritage we still find food with a high fat content appealing. Because of all the additives, especially salt, sugar and fat, we have unwittingly become addicted to aptly name junk food that will kill us. Slowly but surely, it's shortening your life.

Recognise that what you put into your body is of immense importance in enabling your body to heal itself when it gets ill, and in giving it its best chance to function well.

The big bad three

So let's go back to the big bad three. What does sugar do for you? Sugar gives you an instant sense of energy. Too much sugar, however, has a number of side effects. The obvious ones that you will know about will be tooth decay, and, the dangerous one, diabetes. Late-onset adult diabetes is at the highest rate it has ever been in the western world. In America, where obesity is reaching epidemic proportions, the incidence of diabetes is increasing year on year.

Too much salt is not good for you. This is a well-known fact. Back in the 1970s there was a definite correlation proved between salt intake and high blood pressure. Almost every food you will find in nature will contain sufficient salt already. We do not need to add salt, yet restaurants frequently add a lot of salt to dishes to enhance the flavour.

Fat — and there are different types of fat, polyunsaturated being the particular bad boy — plays a huge part in heart disease and obesity.

I designed the 42 days to give you insight and to effect dramatic life-long change, mentally, physically and spiritually. The physical side of your body is going to be directly influenced by your exercise and your diet. **If you eat rubbish then you are not in control of your life.** That is why what you eat is so important. This diet is not about self-denial, it is about self-awareness. If you are not aware of what you eat then you are still asleep and will suffer all the disadvantages of a bad diet, and you won't know it. You will not know how good life can be or how well you can feel, how fit and energetic you should be in the morning, and how quickly you will heal.

I am not somebody who naturally gravitates towards austerity and a severe diet. But this is not about austerity and a severe diet, it is about health and learning the good habits of food.

Stick to good choices

For the purpose of the challenge there are no days off; however, once the challenge is finished I would encourage you one day a week to eat just what you want, be it pizza or fish and chips. As I said, this is not about denial it is about self-awareness.

The word diet has negative connotations. When someone goes on a diet, they feel as though they are being punished – they have done something bad, they are overweight, they are unfit, and because of those states they have to go on a diet. It is like a jail sentence for life, which will deny you the things in life you love, with no parole. I believe dieting is not about denial, it is about self-awareness. So stop thinking diets are bad. A positive approach to eating is vitally important.

I thought long and hard before deciding on what eating plan to recommend. I have examined the different options, looked at current diets from a practical and scientific point of view, and created a simple and straightforward eating plan for the 42 days. It is not based on calorie counting or other measures, but on a healthy and realistic balance of nutrients each day. This eating plan is my recommendation, if you have another diet that you prefer, that you would wish to follow, then as long as it fulfils the criteria of the 42-day food groups then by all means follow your preferred diet/healthy-eating regime.

The 42-day eating plan

- The secret is to eat little and often. Eat six times a day: breakfast, mid-morning, lunch, mid-afternoon, dinner and mid-evening. Choose from 42 different mini-meals, so that you never get bored, based on 8 healthy-eating food groups.
- Eat fresh: fresh fruit, fresh vegetables, fresh meat, poultry and fish.
- As much as possible avoid dairy products, and use skimmed milk.
- No white flour – wholegrain and wholemeal only.
- Where possible always go for the low-carb option.
- Stock up on the foods listed below.

Your 8 healthy-eating food groups

- **Vegetables, especially green vegetables**: they can be steamed, boiled, grilled, roasted or eaten raw. Vegetables are packed with vitamins, and they provide the body with much of its nutritional needs every day. Fresh vegetables (as much as you like) have got to be included in your diet every day.
- **Low-fat diary products**: skimmed milk, low-fat yoghurt, low-fat cottage cheese. The dairy products are a very big source of calcium. Calcium is a vital ingredient in the building of strong bones.
- **Oatmeal**: oatmeal is much overlooked and is often seen as being like wallpaper paste. It is the basic ingredient of porridge and muesli, but before you roll your eyes back and go, 'Oh my gosh, oatmeal every day?' remember it reduces cholesterol, it is high in fibre and is a great slow-burning fuel for the day. It suppresses your appetite by keeping your blood levels normal for longer after you eat it. This stops you having any cravings for a few hours after you've had a bowl of porridge or muesli.
- **Lean meat**: turkey, chicken, other lean meats that are low in fat, and fillet steak. These are high in protein, high in iron, high in zinc, and they promote weight loss because it takes

much longer – and more energy is involved – to digest protein than carbohydrate.

- **Olive oil**: olive oil is a mono-saturated fat, and it's liquid at room temperature, which means it will remain liquid in your body. The saturated fats are solid at room temperature; can you imagine what they may look like in your body? Doesn't bear thinking about. Use olive oil exclusively in this diet. You can use it for gentle shallow frying and salad dressings. It is very high in vitamin E and it helps fight heart disease and high blood pressure. And because of its fat content it makes you feel fuller for longer after you have ingested it.

- **Wholegrain breads and cereals**: very high in fibre, which encourages low insulin levels, which keeps you from storing fat. Some diets say no carbohydrates whatsoever. I don't agree with that. You need carbohydrate in your diet, that's a fact.

- **Nuts**: hazelnuts, almonds and brazil nuts, very high in protein, very high in fibre, full of vitamin E and full of saturated fat. Similar to olive oil they makes you feel full. They are the ultimate in snack foods. A small handful of almonds in the afternoon or in the mid-morning will take away any cravings you may have.

- **Berries**: strawberries, raspberries, blueberries, cranberries, they are packed with antioxidants, which help the body fight heart disease and prevent sugar cravings. They are great for you and a great snack.

Here is a suggested selection of meals to get you started. Choose from seven breakfasts, mid-morning snacks, lunches, afternoon snacks, dinners and mid-evening snacks. All of them can be put together very easily.

Perfect breakfasts

Choose from:

1) Bowl of porridge with skimmed milk, a spoonful of honey and a sprinkling of almonds

2) One boiled egg on a slice of wholemeal toast with a grilled tomato
3) Bowl of muesli with skimmed milk, soaked overnight, heat up if desired, add half a chopped banana
4) Egg-white omelette with three eggs, no yolk, with mushrooms lightly fried in olive oil, on a slice of toast
5) One bowl of yoghurt with assorted berries and one chopped banana
6) Two rashers of grilled lean bacon, one boiled egg and a slice of toast
7) One apple, one orange chopped into a bowl of low-fat yoghurt and blended into a smoothie drink.

7 Mid-morning snacks

Choose from:

1) 2oz of almonds
2) An apple or orange
3) 4oz of cottage cheese
4) Carrot sticks
5) 8oz of natural fruit juice, not sweetened
6) Celery stalks
7) 4oz of low-fat yoghurt

7 Lunches

Choose from:

1) Tuna and green salad sandwich
2) Chicken and pitta bread, with spinach, tomato and low-fat mayonnaise
3) Chunky vegetable soup with wholegrain bread
4) Roast vegetable salad sandwich

5) Poached salmon salad
6) Grilled fish and salad
7) Turkey breast sandwich with chopped onion, mayonnaise and lettuce

7 Mid-afternoon snacks

Choose from:

1) 2oz of almonds or other nuts
2) 4oz cold roast vegetables
3) Apple or orange
4) 4oz cottage cheese
5) 4oz low-fat yoghurt and diced pineapple
6) Small banana
7) Eight strawberries

7 Dinners

Choose from:

1) 6oz fillet steak with roast vegetables
2) Fresh tuna, grilled, with salad of mixed leaves, tomatoes, celery and balsamic vinegar dressing
3) Turkey burger made from fresh minced turkey, lettuce, tomato, low-fat mayonnaise, with fried mushrooms and wholegrain bread
4) Roast mackerel with vegetables and potato
5) Chicken salad with low-fat mayonnaise
6) Roast chicken and assorted roast vegetables
7) Grilled salmon with carrots, peas and spinach

Evening snacks

Choose from:

1) 10oz hot chocolate with skimmed milk
2) Assorted fruit with low-fat yoghurt
3) Banana smoothie with skimmed milk
4) Mixed berries and yoghurt
5) Half melon with yoghurt or berries
6) Low fat ice-cream or sorbet
7) 2oz of nuts

Throughout the day you can have as much herbal tea, water or raw vegetables as you like. **But no** salted nuts, snacks, processed food or carbonated drinks.

A snack is exactly that, a small amount of food to subdue one's appetite. **I always feel you should be able to put a snack into the palm of one hand. We should eat in small bites and snacks should be eaten midway between main meals. You should not feel full, rather that you've had enough.** In fact, if you feel you could always eat a little more, then you have definitely had enough.

Within 10 to 12 days you will discover that food cravings will disappear and your tastes will change. Of course you will want the treats of chocolates and ice-cream, and they will come when the challenge finishes. This challenge is about changing your habits and not being a slave to your food, but its master. This eating plan will help you understand and recognise good healthy food and enable you to make healthy choices in the future.

Exercise

10 simple exercises for the 42-Day Challenge

A healthy diet no matter how rigorously followed will not make you fit. **Fitness is achieved through a combination of diet and exercise, with exercise being the operative word here.** Fitness and improved health come from taking active steps towards achieving them. Most people do not take active exercise and consequently do not function physically as well as they could.

There is a correlation between physical fitness and mental strength. Fit people cope with stress much better and are able to concentrate for much longer periods of time. Yet since we were young children at school, when we were being forced by some apparently cruel and heartless PE teacher to take classes, we have associated fitness with negative states of mind: discomfort, fatigue, pain, hardship. We almost never think of fitness or exercise in terms of rewards, we think of them as time-consuming and exhausting.

Any exercise you take is going to benefit you. The more you take, the more you benefit. The 42-Day Challenge requires you to exercise every day. **Combining exercise with your new diet will** significantly accelerate the impact and effectiveness of this challenge and will dramatically impact on your mental state and your ability to perform at higher levels of effectiveness.

As with the diet I am going to suggest an exercise regime that can be followed by just about anyone irrespective of your current physical condition. The only thing that will vary is the amount of effort each person is able to put into it. So whether you are seriously overweight, in your mid-fifties, or an Olympic athlete, the principles remain the same.

I will add one caveat to this fitness programme. If you go to the gym two or three times a week, or run a few times a week, and have already established a fitness or exercise habit, then stick with that if you prefer to. **It is the daily exercise that is important not the specific exercise.** I am suggesting these specific exercises, in the absence of an existing fitness regime, because they are easy, you can do them at home and they are a very good entry level to the world of physical exercise.

Exercise every day – it's a must

Every day you are required to exercise. **On four of the seven days each week it is simple cardiovascular exercise.** I simply want you to raise your heart level and keep it elevated for twenty minutes – the easiest and best way to do this is to walk quicker than you normally walk – put effort into your strides. Early morning works great. If you wish, you may replace the walking with gentle jogging, it is your choice, but four days a week your exercise should be cardiovascular. Make sure that while you are doing this you are able to maintain a conversation. If you can't maintain a conversation it means you are slightly out of breath and may be putting too much of a strain on your system at the early stages of this programme.

On the three remaining days of the week, I want you to do strength training

Strength training is when you create muscular resistance and in so doing encourage the muscle to grow, and improve the tone and quality of the muscle tissue. You burn more energy, you increase your metabolic rate for a longer period after the exercise is over, you burn fat, you get stronger – it's that simple.

Research has shown resistance training burns fat, reduces blood pressure, raises the metabolic rate and is the fastest way to lose weight and get fit. It enables us to tone up the muscles we have, which gives shape to our physique. The good news is you don't have to do a great deal of resistance training to feel the benefits.

The 42 days has a simple set of 10 exercises

There are 10 exercises in this programme. They have been designed to work every muscle group in the body. Some muscles are given extra attention and I will explain why shortly. The important thing is, by doing the exercises in 20 minutes you will raise your heart rate so you'll have the cardiovascular benefit. You will get the blood circulating and you will use all the muscles in your body.

- You do not need weights to perform them; you only need your own body weight.
- They can be done in a room anywhere, so there is no excuse for not doing them.
- The routine is 20 minutes in duration and you do each of the exercises twice.
- One minute per exercise, repeated twice, that's not so hard, is it?
- When you begin, you will quickly tire, possibly within the

first 20 seconds, and that's OK, because gradually your strength and stamina will improve.

- By the end of the 42 days you will use the full minute to its maximum benefit.

Let's use the first exercise as our example here

The first exercise is the trusty push-up. You do as many as you can within the one-minute period. If you need to rest – rest. So if the first time you do the push-up exercise you can only manage three before your arm muscles exhaust themselves, rest for 10 or 15 seconds. Then try to fit in more repetitions before the minute is over. The next time you do the push-up exercise you will now have a target to go for. Previously it was four, the next time you can go for five. The important thing is that you do the exercise properly, that you give 100% and you do not strain yourself to the point of injury. Common sense will tell you when you reach this point.

Work the muscles

The muscle groups that I want to focus on are the quads, which are in your thighs, and your abdominal muscles, where your core strength lies. **When you do a squat it is estimated that you use over 240 separate muscles; the quads are the biggest muscle group in the body. By using them you will increase the rate at which you burn fat and the amount of energy you use.** The exercises have been designed so you can incrementally increase the quality and the quantity you do within one minute. If the first time you do them you can only manage one push-up or one squat that is not important, the important thing is you are trying, you are taking action, you are following the principles of the 42 days. If you only do one push-up and rest for 30 seconds before you try another, that's fine; on the other hand if you do 50 push-ups in the first minute, good for you, this is all about doing your best.

The 10 exercises are as follows:

The push-up

The push-up is a classic and a standard exercise with which you will be familiar. Simply, put your hands about shoulder-width apart and then, keeping your back straight, bend at the elbows until you almost touch the floor with your nose. Then, keeping your body straight, push back up. Breathe in as you go down and breathe out as you push up.

The squat

Keeping your back straight, and your feet about shoulder-width apart and your arms stretched out in front of you, looking straight ahead, lower your body almost as though you were about to sit in a chair. Continue going down until your thighs are parallel to the floor. Hold this position for one second and then return to the upright. Breathing in as you go down, and breathing out as you go up.

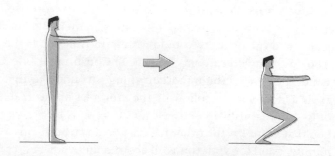

The lunge

This is an excellent exercise for the quads. Standing upright, take a long step forward and then bend the knee of the leading leg and lower the knee of the back leg towards the ground. Return to the starting position and then use the other leg to go forward, lunge and bend.

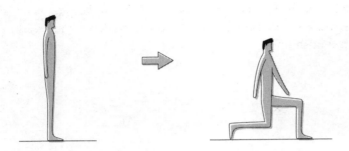

The triceps dip

Putting the palms of your hands on a chair and keeping your legs out from the chair and straight, lower your bottom to the ground. Just before it touches the ground push back up. As you go down breathe in, as you come up breathe out.

The calf raise

Simply stand on a stair holding the banister with one hand and then raise your heels off the ground, keeping your weight balanced on the balls of your feet. Raise your heels as high off the ground as you can go, then lower them down. Do this as many times as you can.

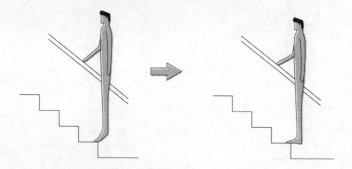

The sit-up

Lying flat on your back, put your hands behind your head and, leaning forward from the waist, sit up. As you come up breathe out, as you go down breathe in.

The step-up

On the staircase in your house, or on a small step, step up and step down, alternating your leading leg.

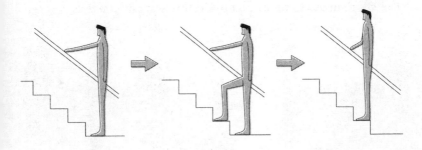

The bridge

Get into the push-up position but instead of using your hands rest your weight on your forearms so your elbows and the palms of your hands are now on the ground. Move your weight slightly forward, so that the majority of your weight is over your forearms, and hold this position as long as you can. Each time you do it, try to increase the length of time until you can hold this position for 60 seconds.

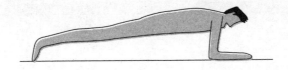

The leg raise

Lying on your back with your hands underneath your buttocks, lift both your legs off the ground about six inches. Once you have held this position extend your legs wide then bring them back together. Do this as many times as you can before stopping to rest.

The chest raise

Lying flat on the ground with your arms out ahead of you, rather like Superman, lift your arms and shoulders as far off the ground as possible, keeping your hips fixed to the ground. You will find that to begin with your shoulders may not move very much at all but this exercise is designed to help develop your back muscles. Developing your back muscles with your abdominal muscles will give you excellent core strength.

As you become more accomplished at doing these exercises you will find that your stamina will increase and indeed so will your strength. You will always be tired at the end of the 20 minutes because even though your fitness and stamina levels will increase; you will be able to exercise longer, you will always go to the point of fatigue.

When you compare how many exercises you can do at the end of the 42 days with the notes you took on day one, I think **you will see an increase of over 100% and be feeling a lot better**, and I have no doubt people will notice the difference in you.

Now What?

You've completed the 42 days, and you have changed. So what's happened? I believe and hope that you will be happier and that your self-esteem has increased dramatically, that you have lost weight and become significantly fitter. Your eating habits are better than they've ever been in your life and your time-management has become efficient, but most importantly you're different as a person. You've broken the failure habit and you understand how the failure habit worked in your life before. You will have reflected more upon the impact of body, mind and spirit and how they are all part of the same system.

The purpose of the challenge has been to get you to take control of your life, how you think, how you feel and how you behave. To understand that your success is in your hands.

People have written telling me of the outcome of life changes. For some they are profound, for some they are simple, all are transformational. The critical thing is they all understood that they can change. As you move forward you can do the challenge again at different times to set new inspiring goals for yourself. I'll let you in on a secret: it gets easier and easier. The challenge puts you back in control and enables you to focus on the life you want to live, and not a life of regrets and frustration.

Please write to me and let me know of your successes, or if you require extra assistance or information visit: **www.42Daychallenge. com.**

> ## As a result of the 42 days you have grown. I hope you have come to an understanding that you are in control of your life

Our lives are not simply about acquisition and material gain, they are equally about love and self-fulfilment. Life is about being happy and finding our joy in ourselves and in the world around us. **You can use the principles you've learned in the 42 days to achieve any goal you set yourself as long as it is within the realms of the realistic.** I've often said this before – I don't believe that by setting the goal to fly unaided, you'll be able to fly, because that does not align with the natural laws of the universe. **So too with your life, select for yourself goals and aspirations that are realistic, and make them happen.**

Because when you believe you can, you will.

Robin Sieger

Robin Sieger is the founder of Sieger International Ltd with offices in London (UK), and Charlotte NC (USA). The company has built an international reputation amongst businesses as a powerful catalyst for performance transformation.

Sieger International helps individuals and organisations release their potential through the creation of a success culture, turning potential into profit. It has a wide range of clients – from start-up entrepreneurs through to FTSE 100 companies.

In addition to the business arena, Sieger International runs the 100% NBW™ programme for schools enabling children to develop their self-worth and inspire them to learn and apply the principles behind personal success.

An acknowledged world class keynote speaker, Robin Sieger is noted for his humour and his ability to inspire, motivate, and transform audiences around the world. He was one of the first three speakers in the UK to be awarded a fellowship in recognition of his achievements. His corporate training, consulting and speaking clients include British Airways, British Telecom, General Motors, Ford Motor Co., HSBC, IBM, Microsoft, McDonald's, Nokia, Coca-Cola and Zurich Financial.

Natural Born Winners has been sold in over sixty countries worldwide and in 2004 was turned into a television series.

For further information on Robin Sieger and Sieger International Ltd's training and consulting services, please contact:

Sieger International Ltd
Molasses House
Plantation Wharf
London SW11 3TH

0845 2305400

www.siegerinternational.com

robin@siegerinternational.com